PIANO BALLADS
IN EASY KEYS

"Piano Ballads in Easy Keys" include no more th... ...or one flat in the **key signature**. The key signature appears on the left sid... ...to the clef signs.

no sharps or flats   one s...   one flat: B♭

all Fs are played as ...   Bs are played as B♭

Sometimes **accidentals** appear. Accidentals are sharps and flats not in the key signature. An accidental alters a specific note in a particular measure. The next bar line or a natural sign (♮) cancels an accidental.

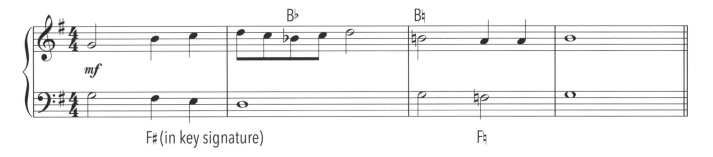

F# (in key signature)   F♮

ISBN 978-1-70514-325-4

7777 W. BLUEMOUND RD. P.O. BOX 13819 MILWAUKEE, WI 53213

Visit Hal Leonard Online at
www.halleonard.com

Contact us:
Hal Leonard
7777 West Bluemound Road
Milwaukee, WI 53213
Email: info@halleonard.com

In Europe, contact:
Hal Leonard Europe Limited
42 Wigmore Street
Marylebone, London, W1U 2RN
Email: info@halleonardeurope.com

In Australia, contact:
Hal Leonard Australia Pty. Ltd.
4 Lentara Court
Cheltenham, Victoria, 3192 Australia
Email: info@halleonard.com.au

BEAUTIFUL

Words and Music by
LINDA PERRY

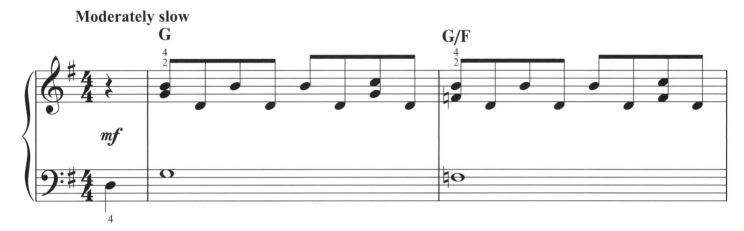

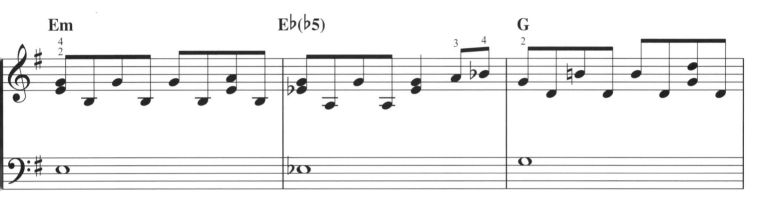

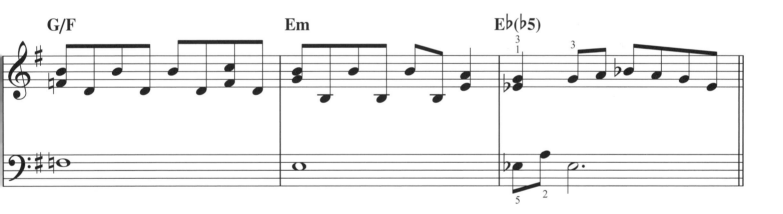

Ev - 'ry day is so won - der - ful, then sud - den -
To all your friends you're de - lir - i - ous. So con -

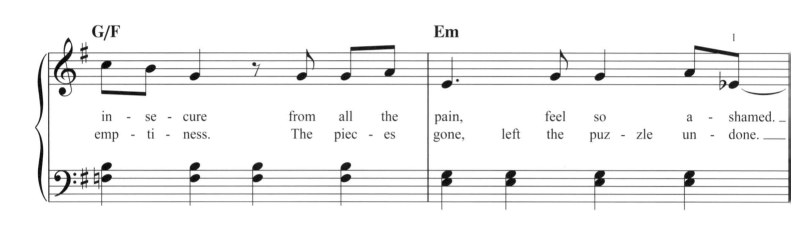

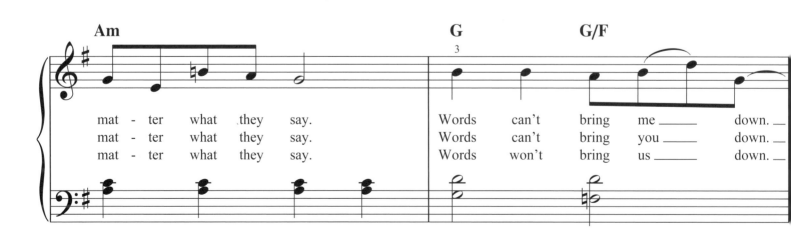

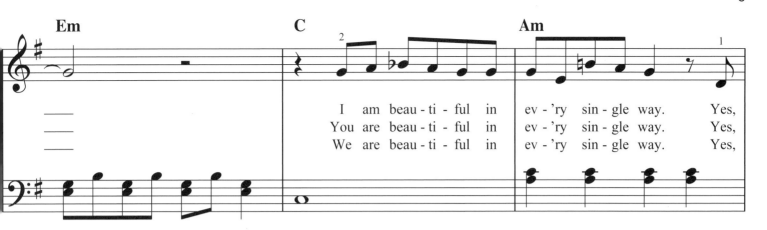

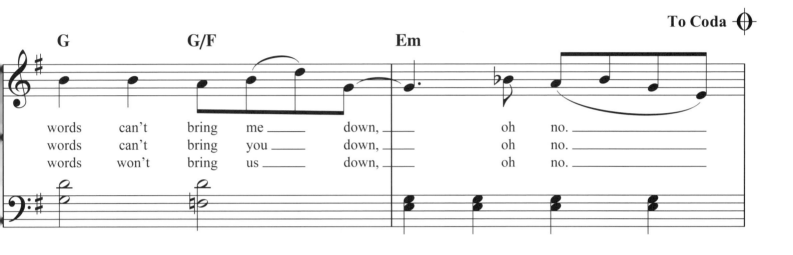

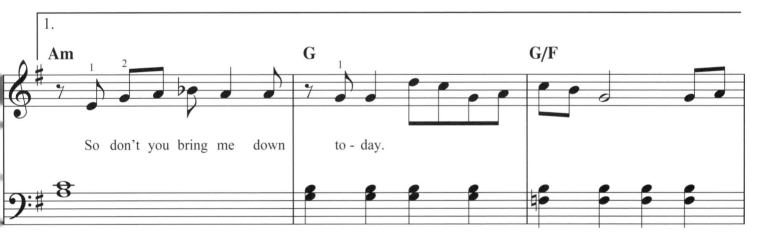

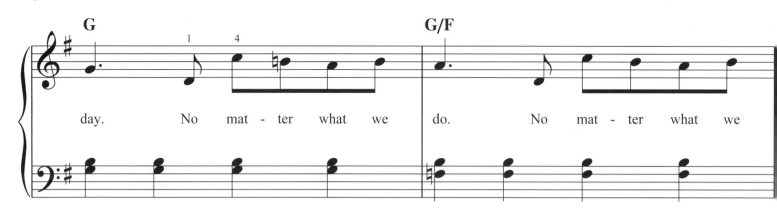

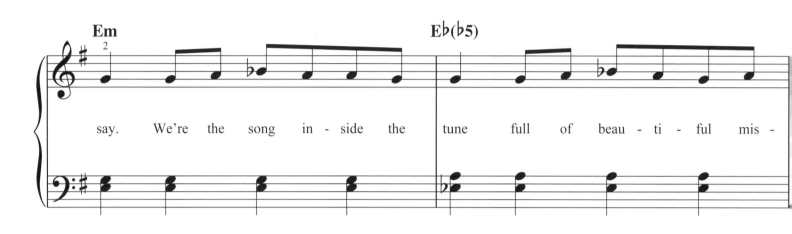

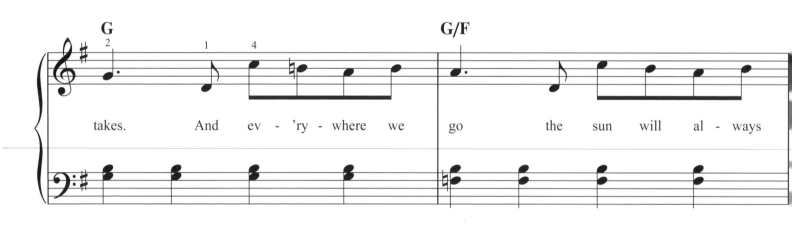

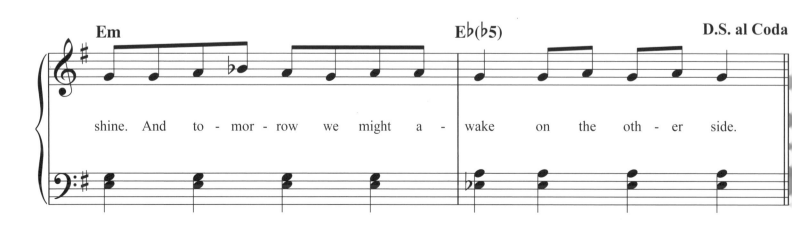

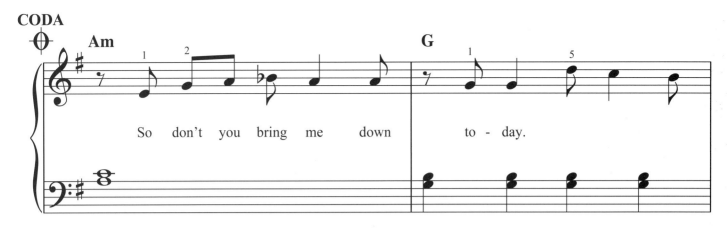

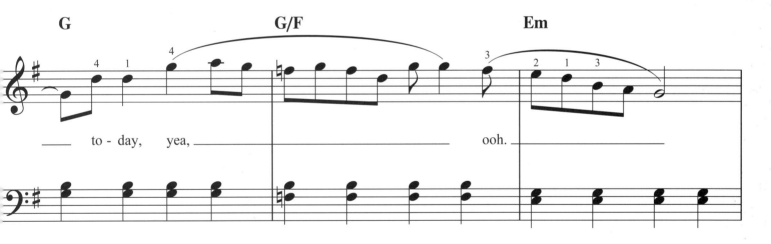

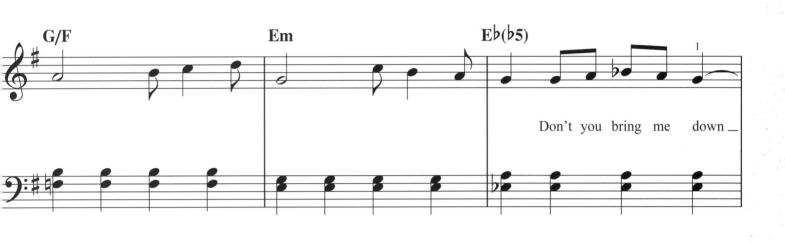

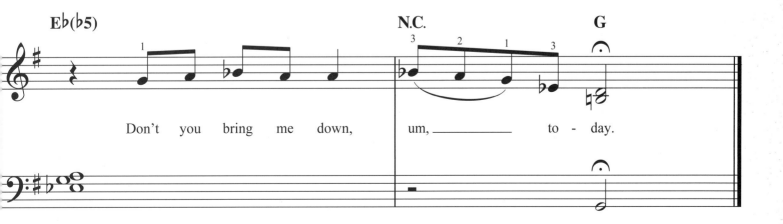

BEAUTY AND THE BEAST

from BEAUTY AND THE BEAST

Music by ALAN MENKEN
Lyrics by HOWARD ASHMAN

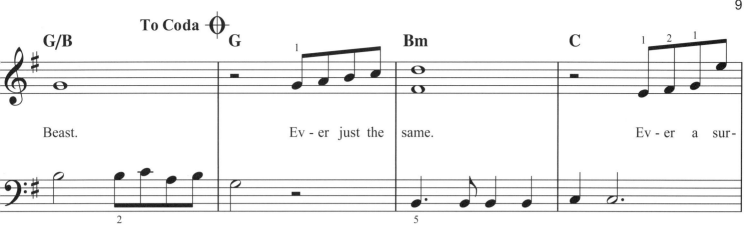

Beast. Ev - er just the same. Ev - er a sur-

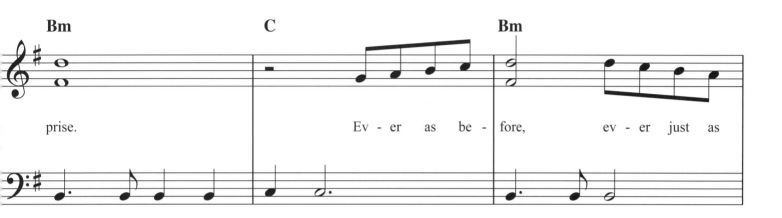

prise. Ev - er as be - fore, ev - er just as

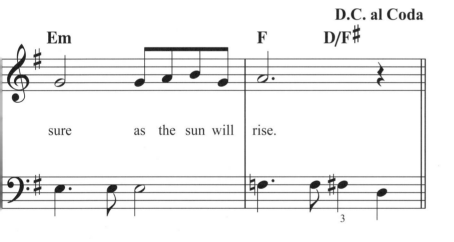

sure as the sun will rise.

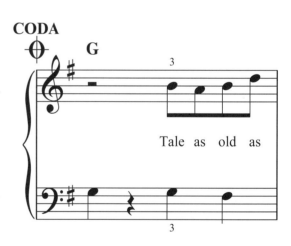

Tale as old as

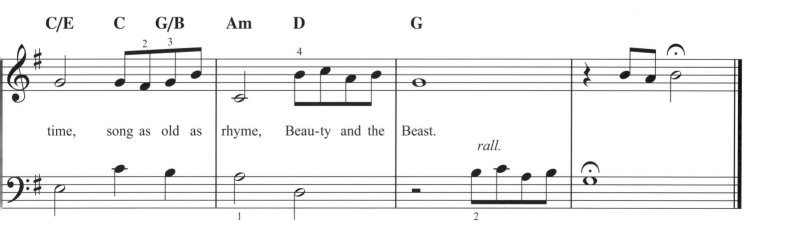

time, song as old as rhyme, Beau-ty and the Beast.

BRIDGE OVER TROUBLED WATER

Words and Music by
PAUL SIMON

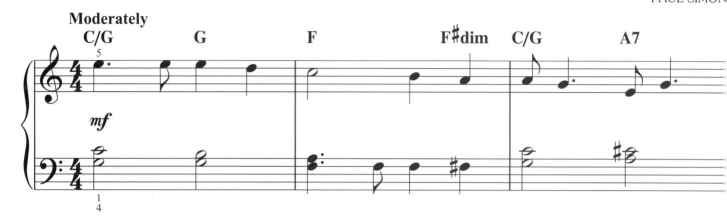

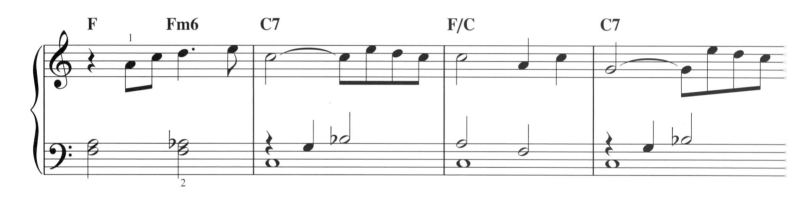

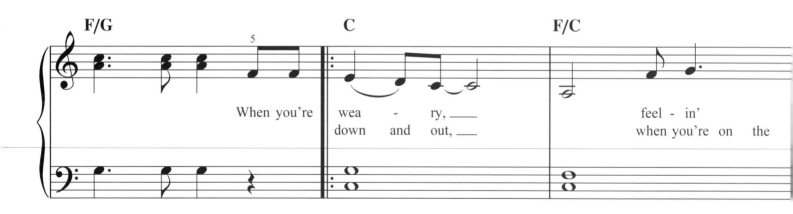

When you're wea - ry, ____ feel - in'
down and out, ____ when you're on the

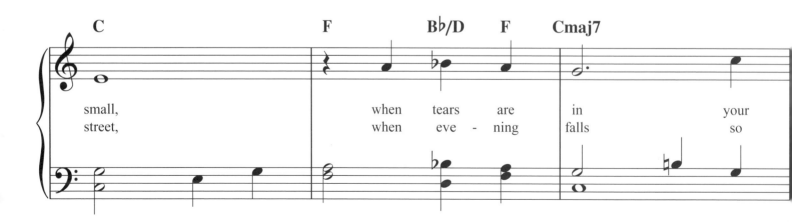

small, when tears are in your
street, when eve - ning falls so

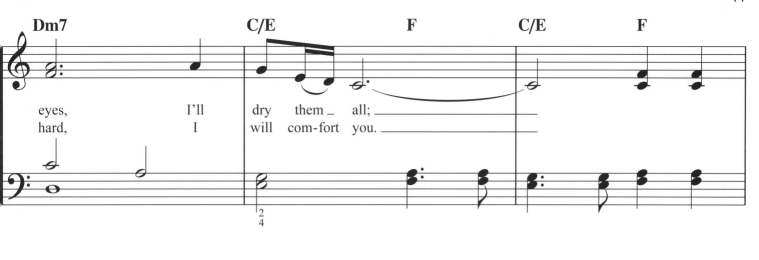

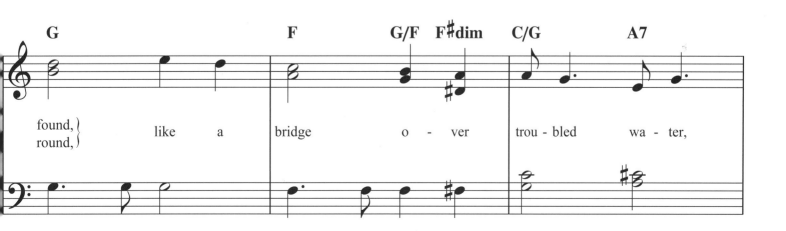

12

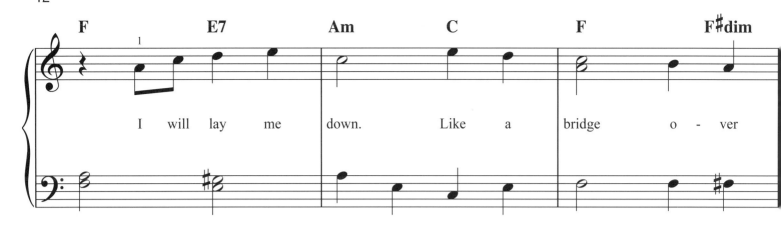

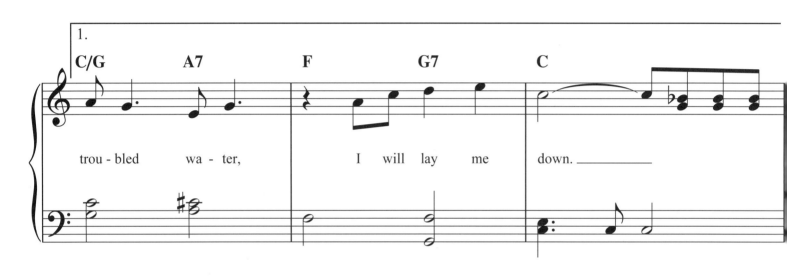

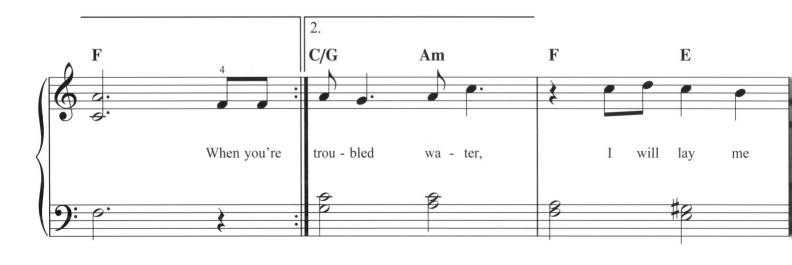

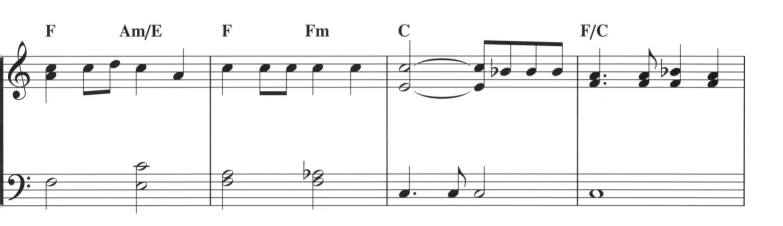

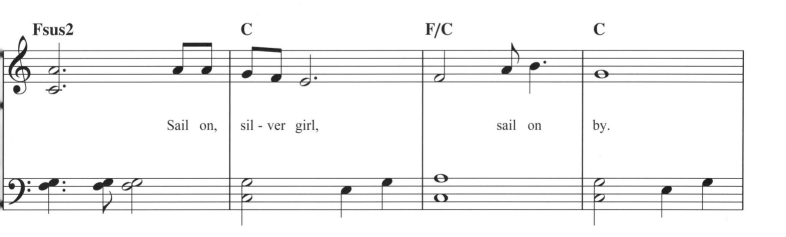

down.

Sail on, sil - ver girl, sail on by.

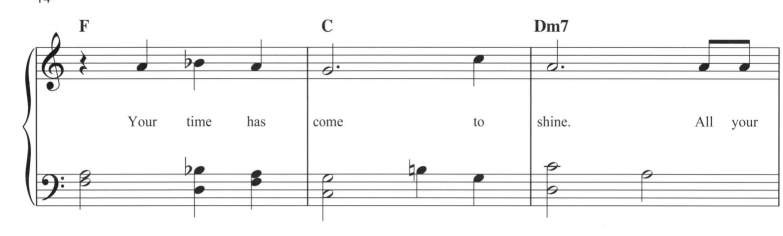

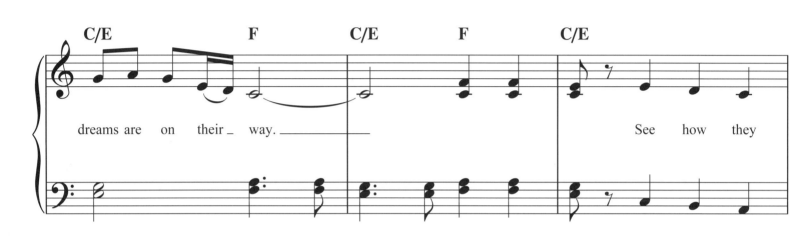

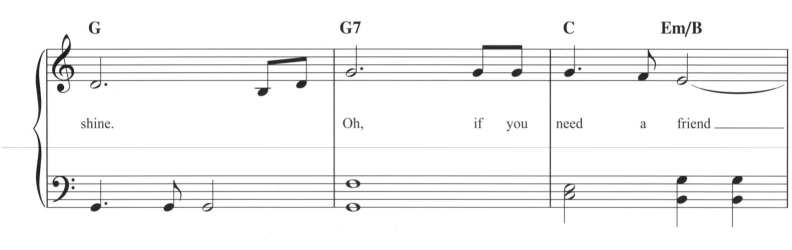

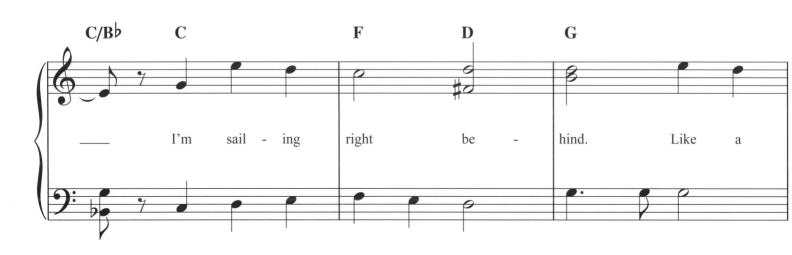

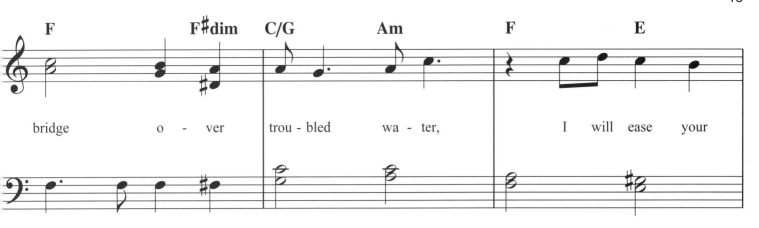

bridge o - ver trou - bled wa - ter, I will ease your

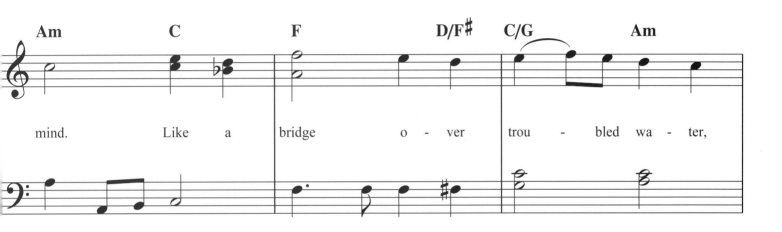

mind. Like a bridge o - ver trou - bled wa - ter,

I will ease your mind.

rit.

CANDLE IN THE WIND

Words and Music by ELTON JOHN
and BERNIE TAUPIN

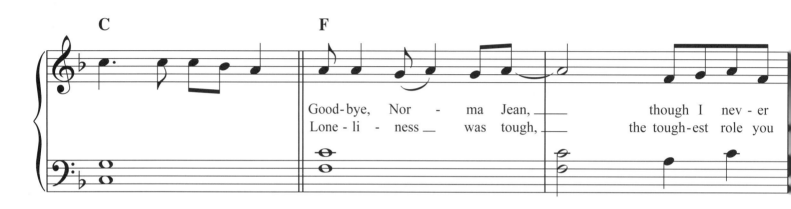

Good-bye, Nor - ma Jean, ___ though I nev - er
Lone - li - ness ___ was tough, ___ the tough-est role you

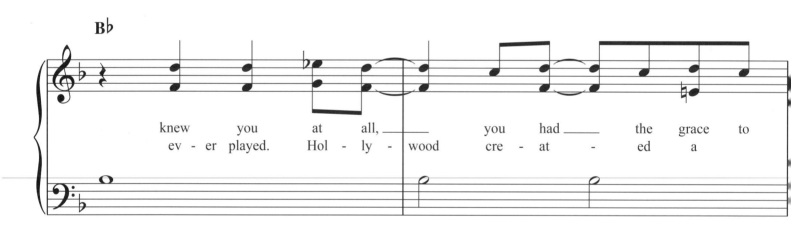

knew you at all, ___ you had ___ the grace to
ev - er played. Hol - ly - wood cre - at - ed a

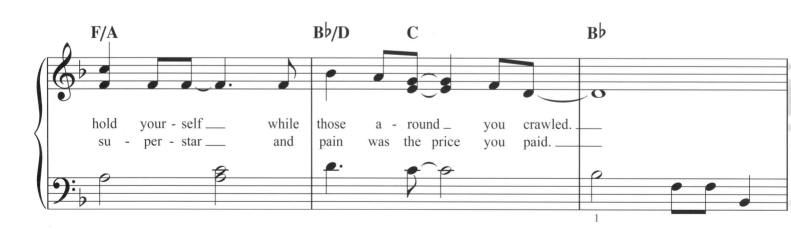

hold your - self ___ while those a - round ___ you crawled.
su - per - star ___ and pain was the price you paid. ___

They crawled out of the wood-work _____ and they whis-pered
E - ven when you died, _____ oh, the

in - to _____ your brain, _____ they set you on a tread - mill _____ and they
press still hound - ed you, _____ all the pa - pers had _____ to say was that

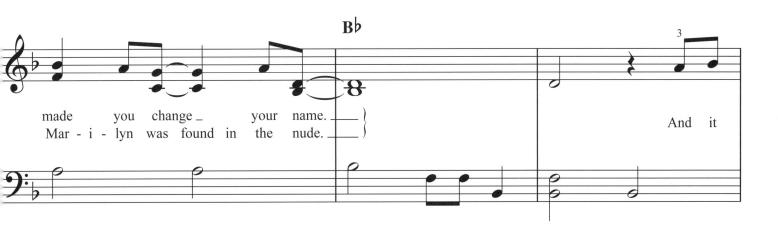

made you change ___ your name. _____
Mar - i - lyn was found in the nude. _____

And it

seems to me you lived your life _____ like a can - dle in _____ the wind. __

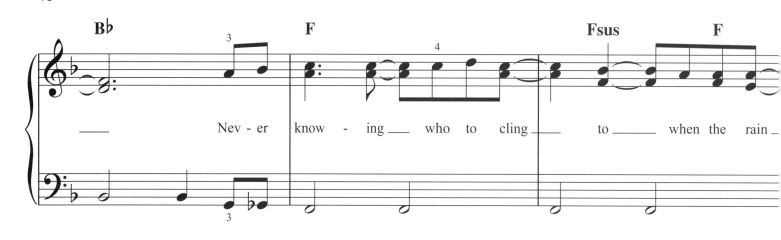

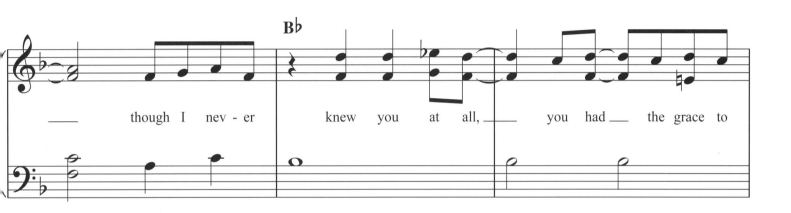

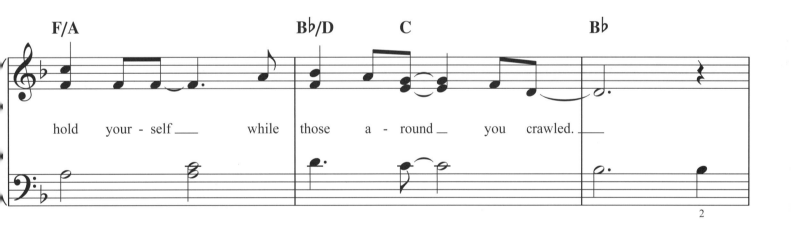

twen - ty - sec - ond row ___ who sees you as some-thing more than sex - u - al, ___ more than

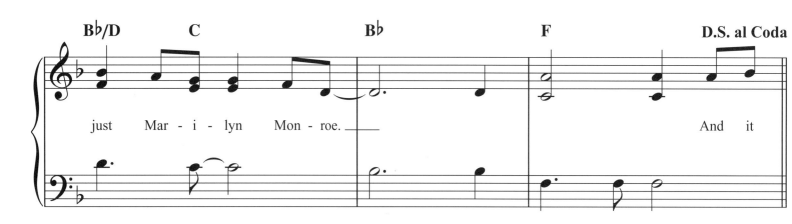

just Mar - i - lyn Mon - roe. ___ And it

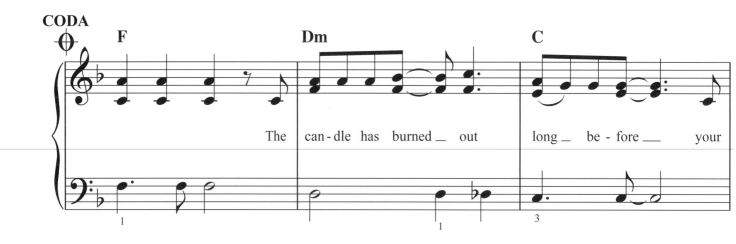

The can - dle has burned ___ out long ___ be - fore ___ your

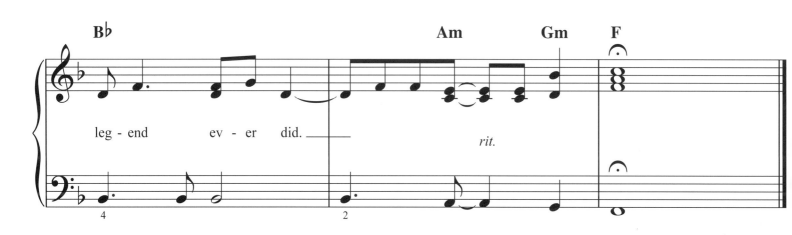

leg - end ev - er did. ___ *rit.*

CAN YOU FEEL THE LOVE TONIGHT

from THE LION KING

Music by ELTON JOHN
Lyrics by TIM RICE

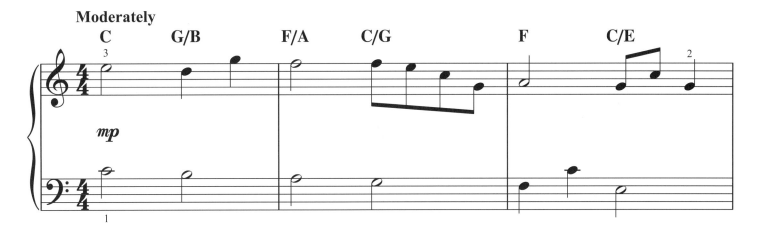

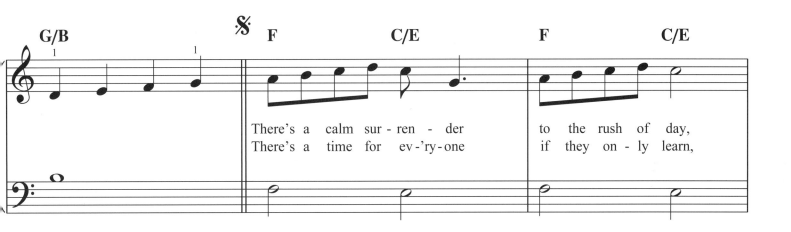

There's a calm sur-ren-der to the rush of day,
There's a time for ev-'ry-one if they on-ly learn,

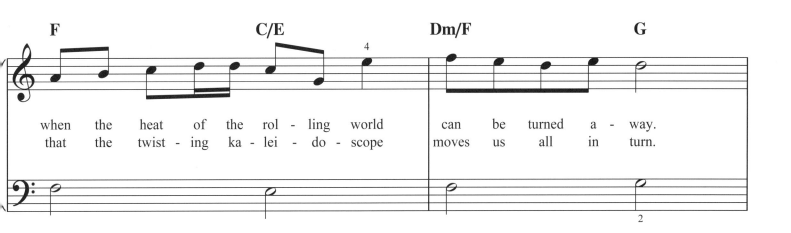

when the heat of the rol-ling world can be turned a-way.
that the twist-ing ka-lei-do-scope moves us all in turn.

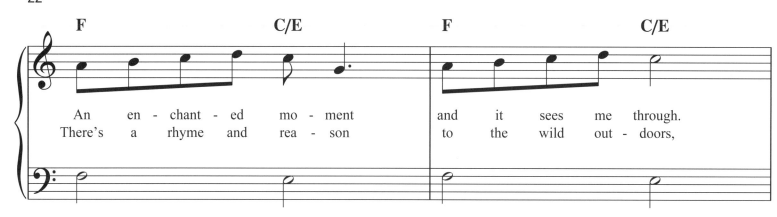

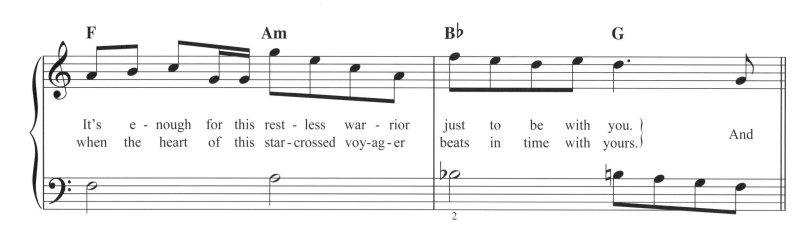

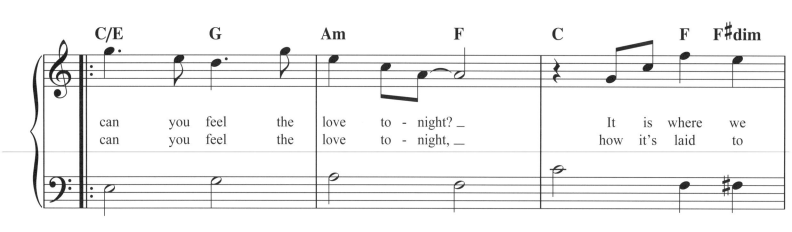

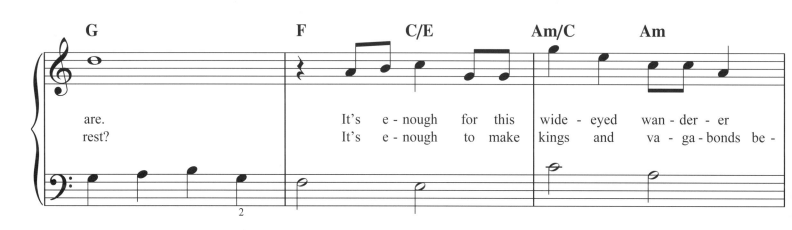

FIELDS OF GOLD

Music and Lyrics by
STING

Flowing, moderately

Am7

You'll re-

Am7   F

mem - ber   me   when the   west wind   moves   up - on   the   fields   of
stay with   me,   will you   be my   love   a - mong   the   fields   of

C   Am7   F   C

bar - ley.   You'll for - get the   sun   in his   jeal - ous   sky   as we
bar - ley?   We'll for - get the   sun   in his   jeal - ous   sky   as we

walk in fields _ of gold. _____
lie in fields _ of gold. _____

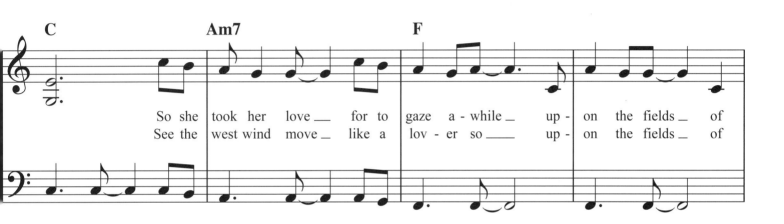

So she took her love _ for to gaze a - while _ up - on the fields _ of
See the west wind move _ like a lov - er so ____ up - on the fields _ of

bar - ley. In his arms she fell ____ as her hair came down _ a -
bar - ley. Feel her bod - y rise ____ when you kiss her mouth _ a -

mong the fields _ of gold. Will you
mong the fields _ of gold. I nev - er made

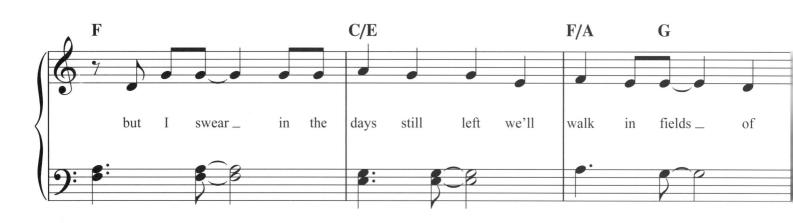

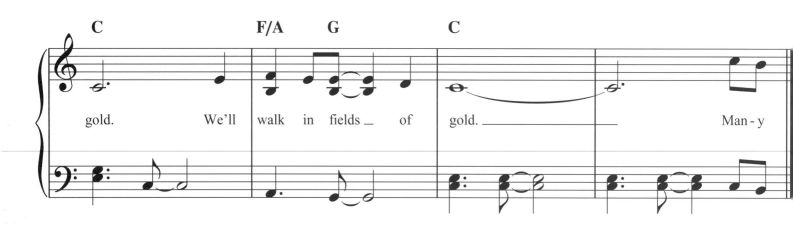

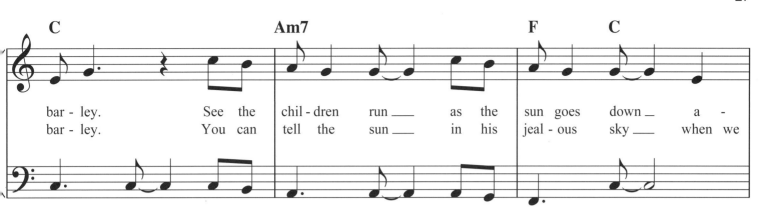

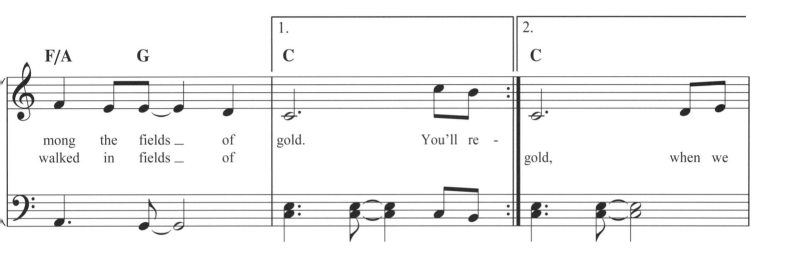

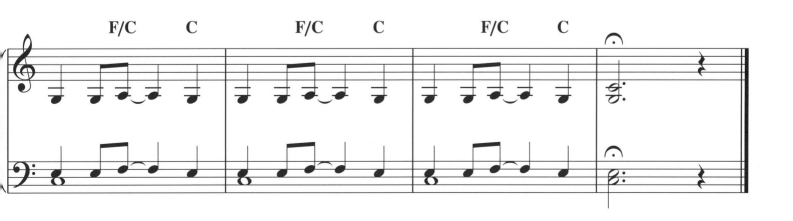

GO THE DISTANCE

from HERCULES

Music by ALAN MENKEN
Lyrics by DAVID ZIPPEL

Slow Ballad

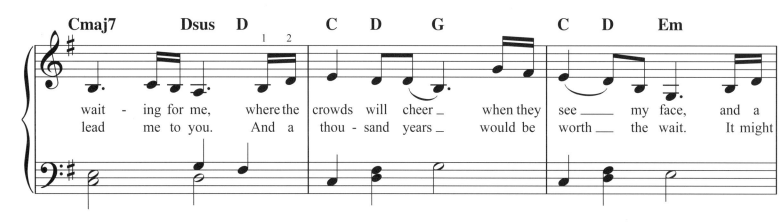

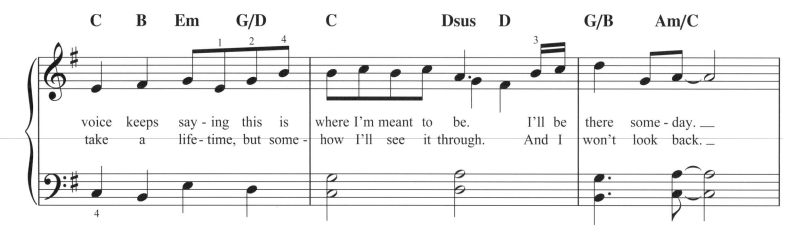

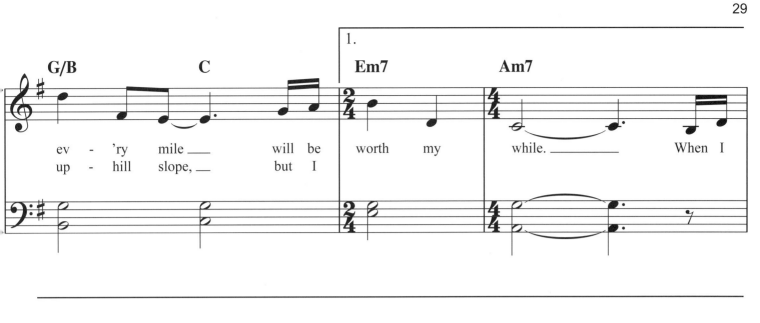

ev - 'ry mile ____ will be worth my while. ____ When I
up - hill slope, ___ but I

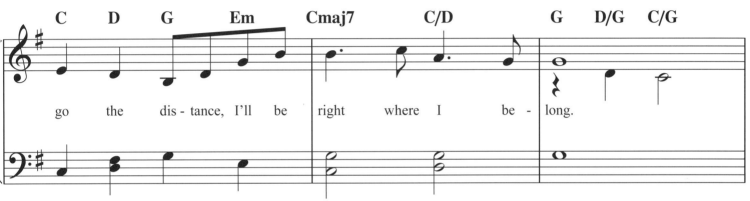

go the dis - tance, I'll be right where I be - long.

Down an won't lose hope __ till I go the dis - tance and my

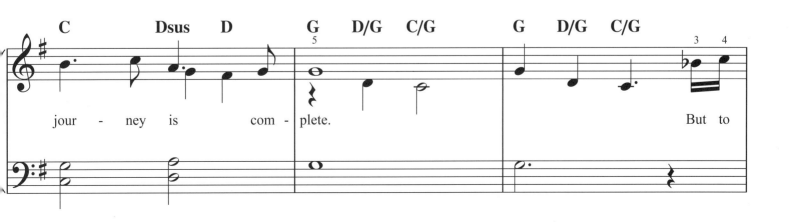

jour - ney is com - plete. But to

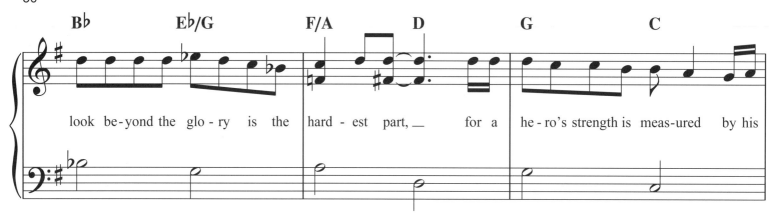

look be-yond the glo-ry is the hard-est part, ___ for a he-ro's strength is meas-ured by his

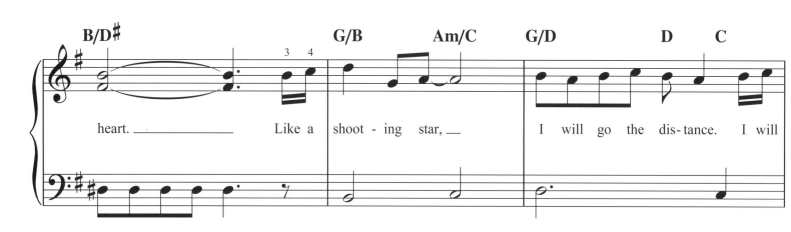

heart. _____ Like a shoot-ing star, ___ I will go the dis-tance. I will

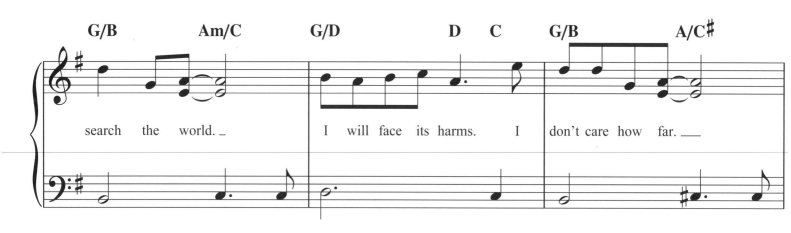

search the world. _ I will face its harms. I don't care how far. ___

I can go the dis-tance till I find my he-ro's wel-come wait-ing

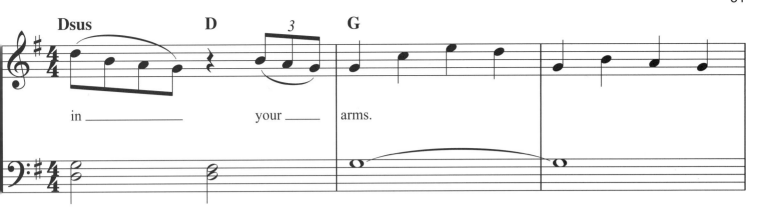

in your arms.

I will

search the world. I will face it's harms till I

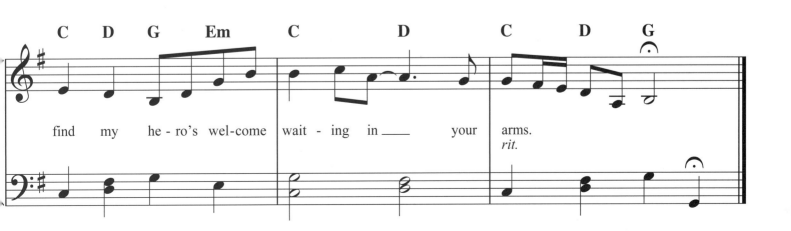

find my he-ro's wel-come wait-ing in your arms.
rit.

GROW OLD WITH ME

Words and Music by
JOHN LENNON

Moderately, with expression

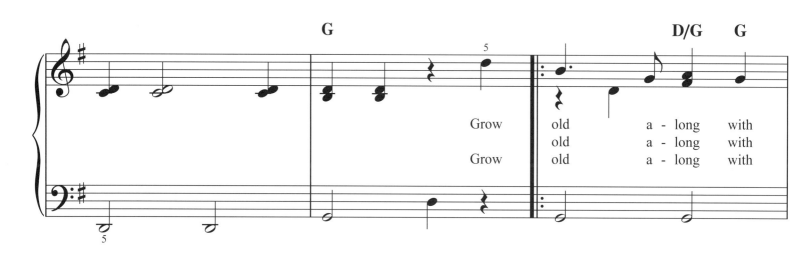

Grow old a - long with
old a - long with
Grow old a - long with

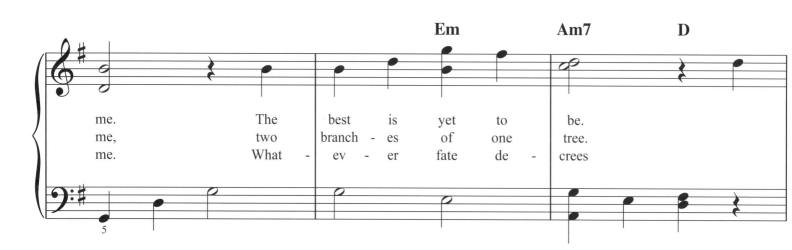

me. The best is yet to be.
me, two branch - es of one tree.
me. What - ev - er fate de - crees

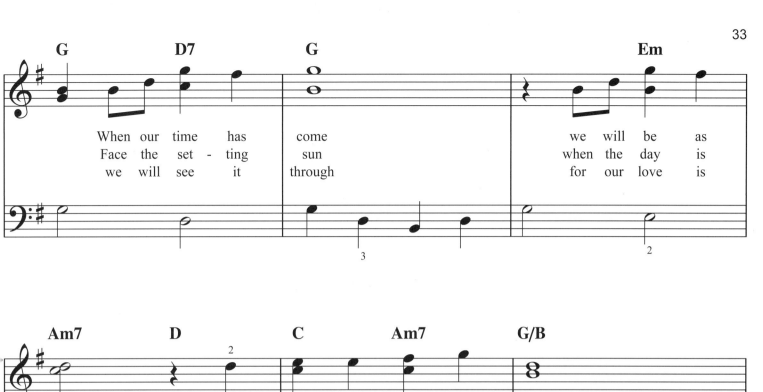

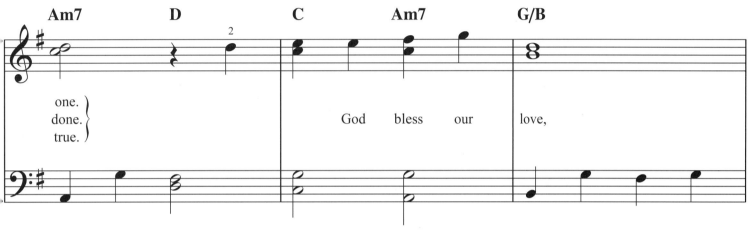

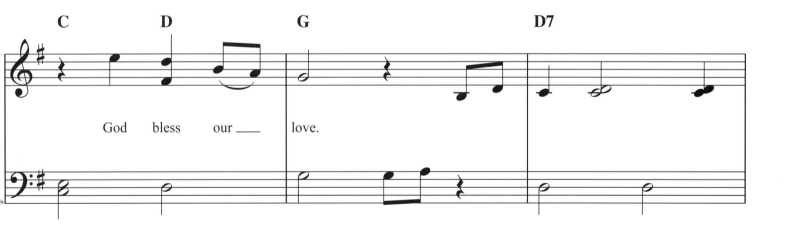

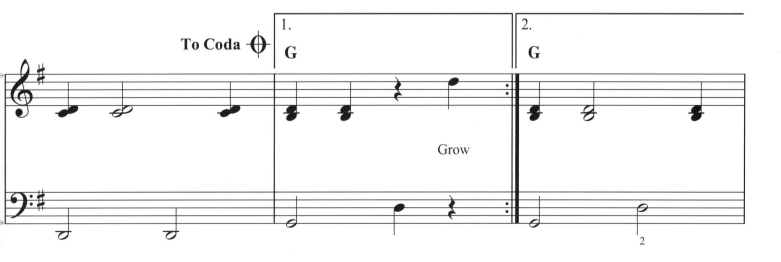

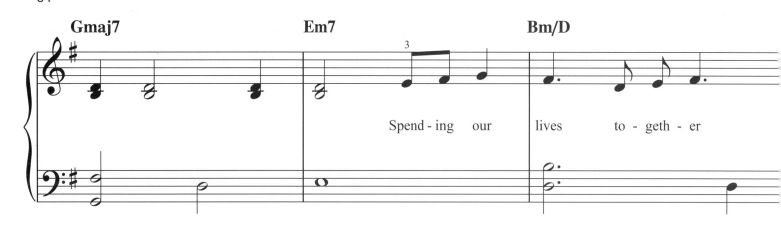

Spend - ing our lives to - geth - er

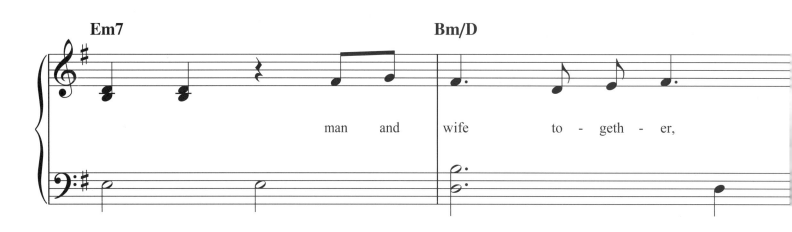

man and wife to - geth - er,

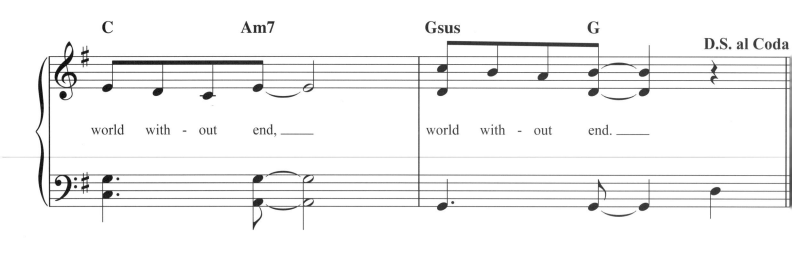

world with - out end, _____ world with - out end. _____

D.S. al Coda

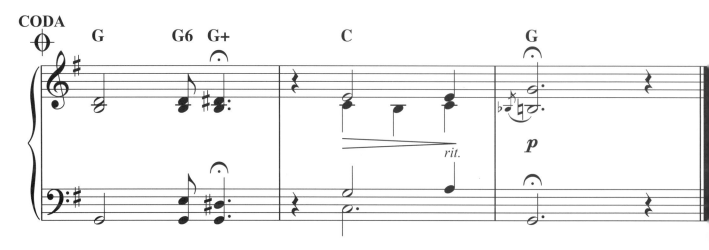

CODA

rit.

p

HELLO

Words and Music by
LIONEL RICHIE

Slow Ballad

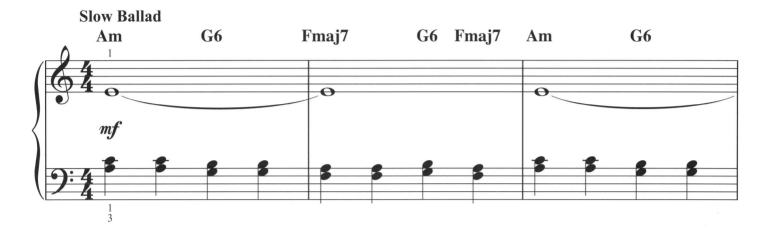

I've been a-lone with you in-side my ____ mind, ____ and
long to see the sun-light in your ____ hair, ____ and

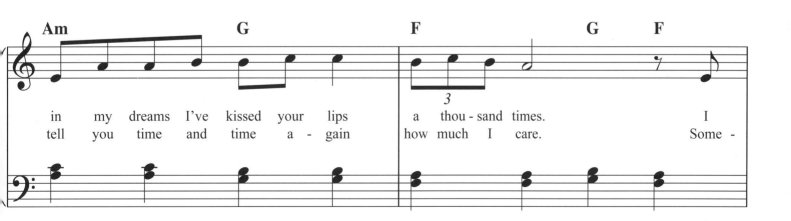

in my dreams I've kissed your lips a thou-sand times. I
tell you time and time a-gain how much I care. Some-

36

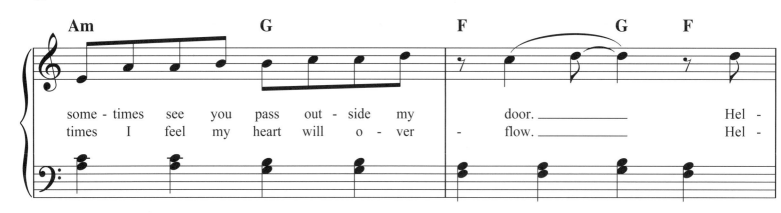

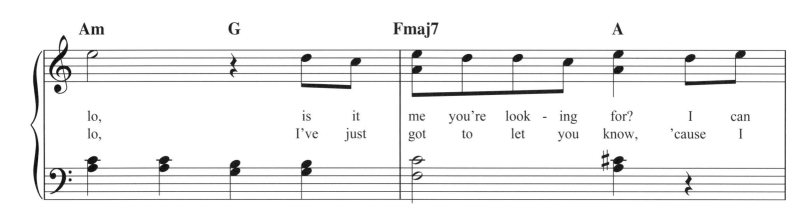

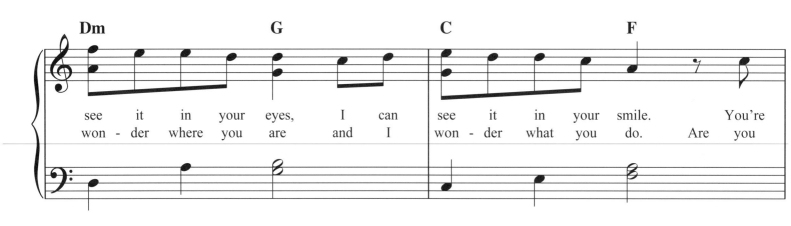

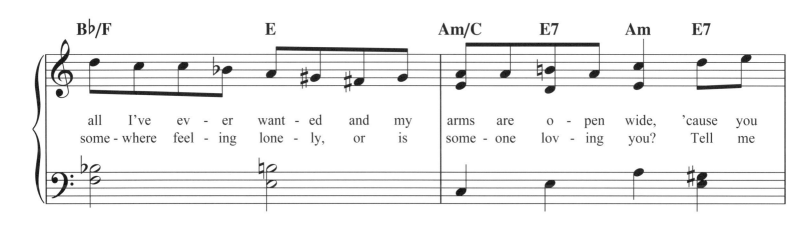

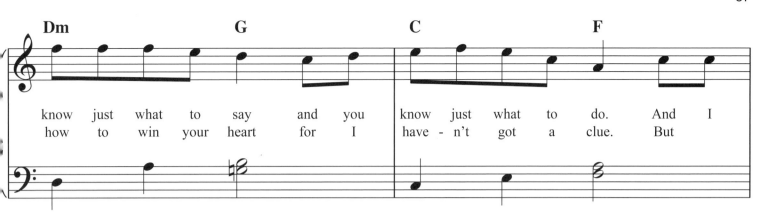

know just what to say and you know just what to do. And I
how to win your heart for I have - n't got a clue. But

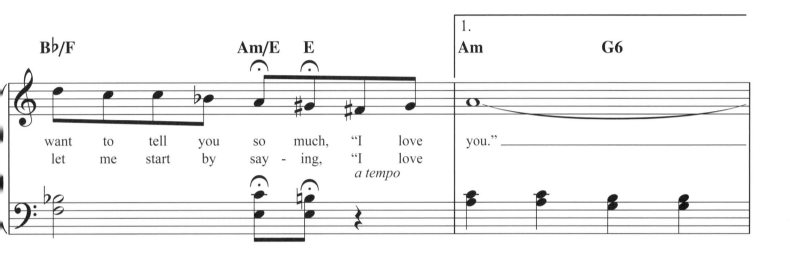

want to tell you so much, "I love you."
let me start by say - ing, "I love

a tempo

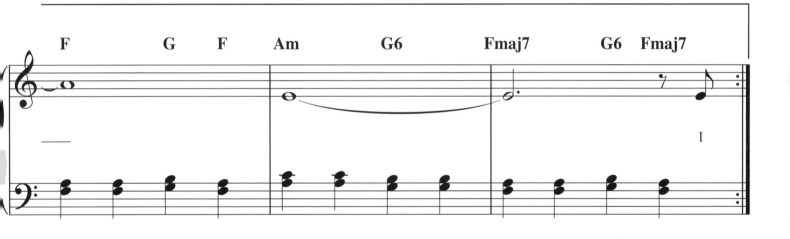

I

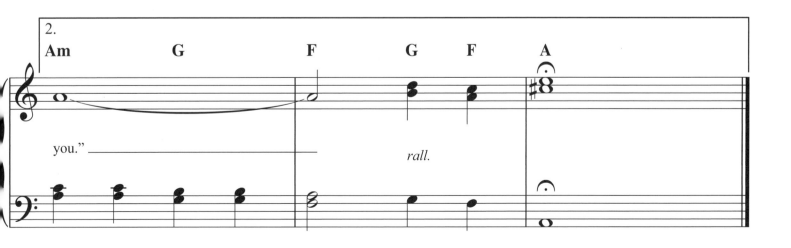

you."

rall.

HERO

Words and Music by MARIAH CAREY
and WALTER AFANASIEFF

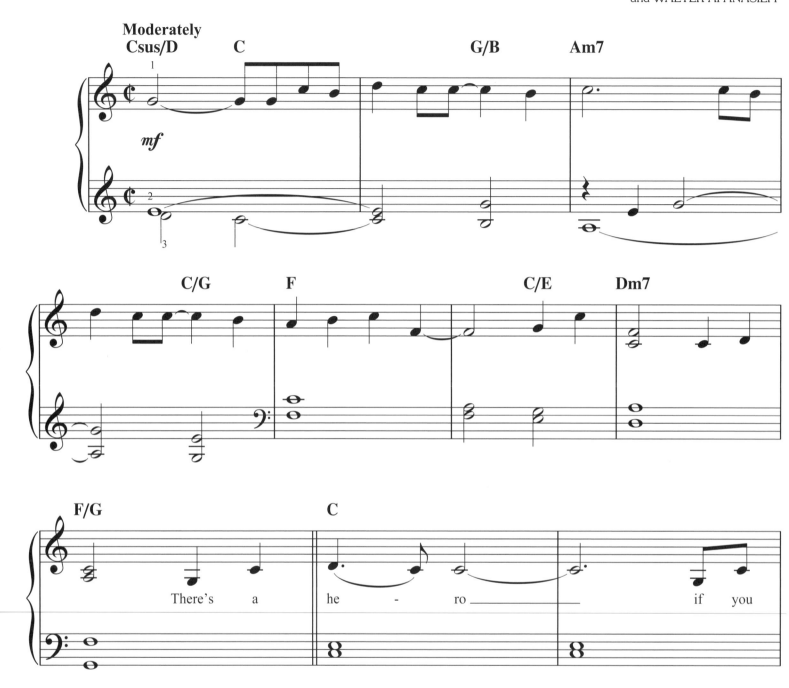

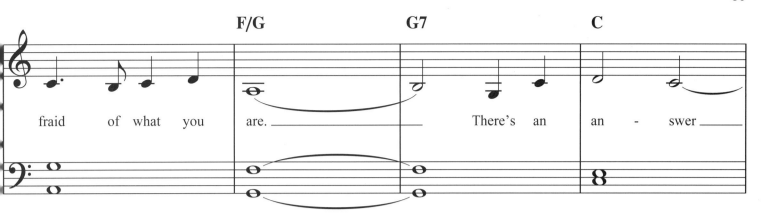

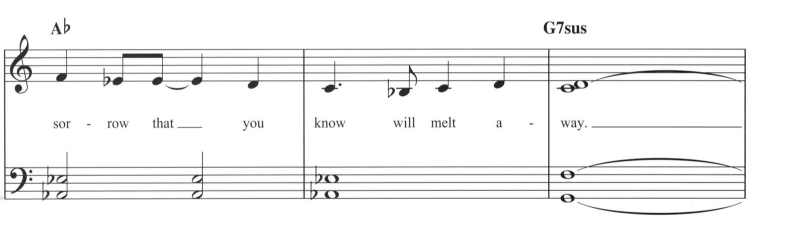

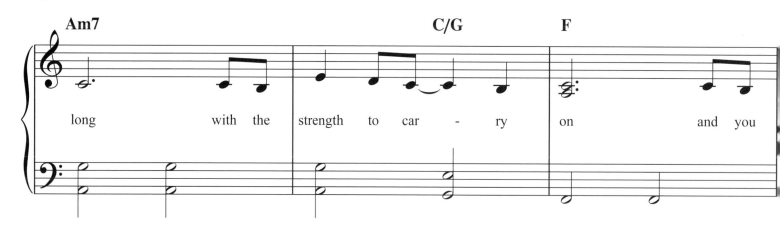

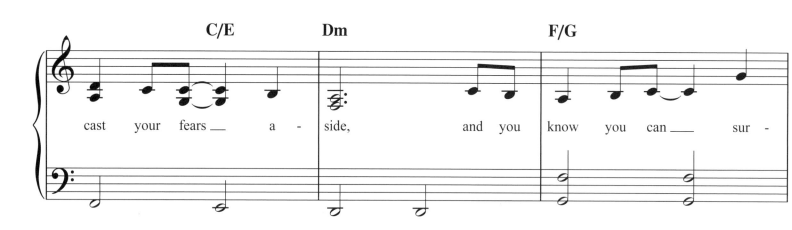

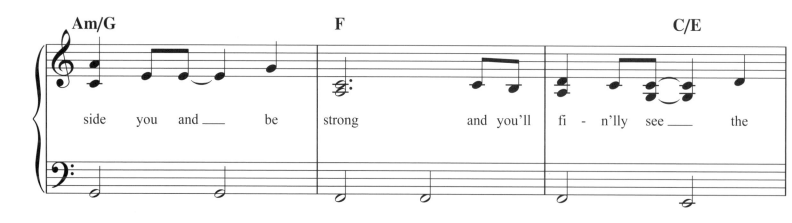

truth that a he - ro lies ____ in you.

That a he - ro lies in you.
molto rall.   *a tempo*

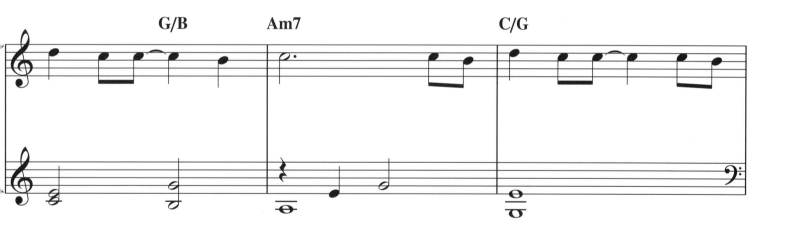

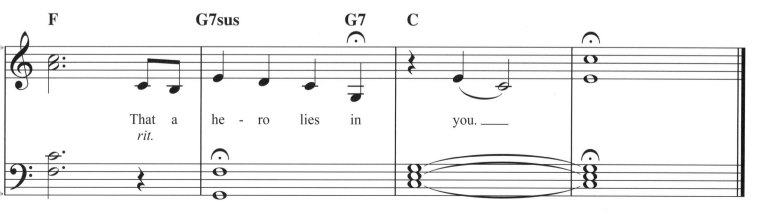

That a he - ro lies in you. ____
rit.

HOW AM I SUPPOSED TO LIVE WITHOUT YOU

Words and Music by MICHAEL BOLTON
and DOUG JAMES

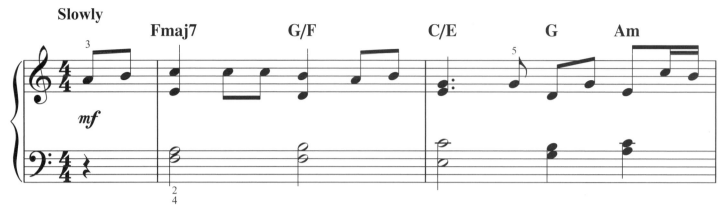

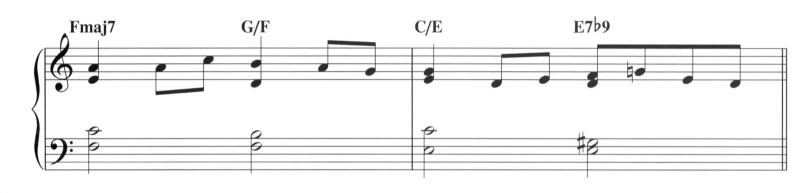

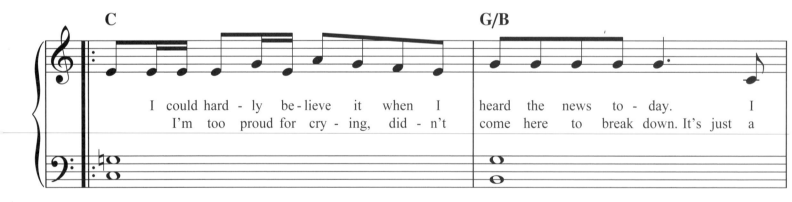

I could hard - ly be - lieve it when I heard the news to - day. I
I'm too proud for cry - ing, did - n't come here to break down. It's just a

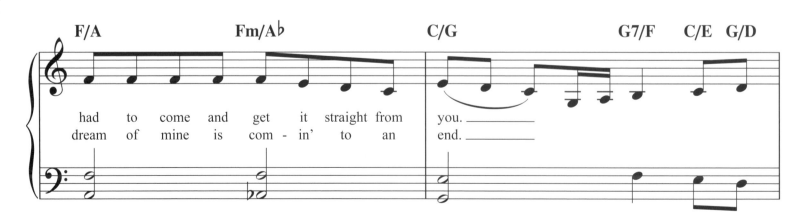

had to come and get it straight from you. _____
dream of mine is com - in' to an end. _____

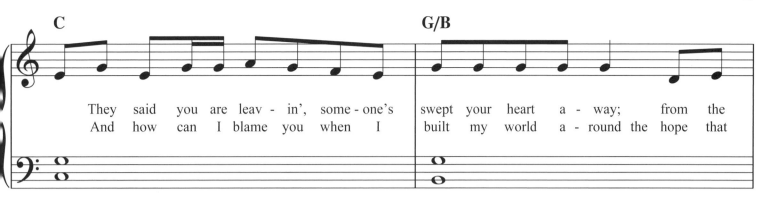

They said you are leav - in', some - one's swept your heart a - way; from the
And how can I blame you when I built my world a - round the hope that

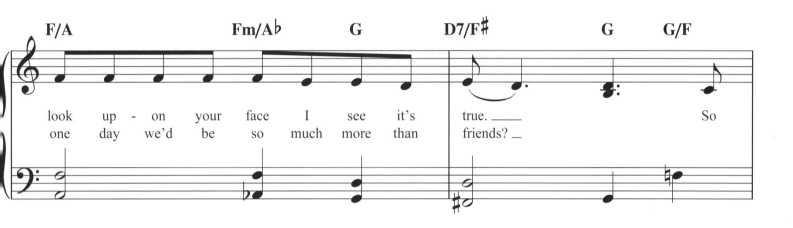

look up - on your face I see it's true. _____ So
one day we'd be so much more than friends? _

tell me all a - bout it, tell me 'bout the plans you're mak - in'.
I don't want to know the price I'm gon - na pay for dream - in'.
I don't want to know the price I'm gon - na pay for dream - in',

Tell me one thing more be - fore I go. _____ Tell me, how am I sup-posed to live with-
E - ven now it's more than I can take. ___
now that your dream has come true. ___

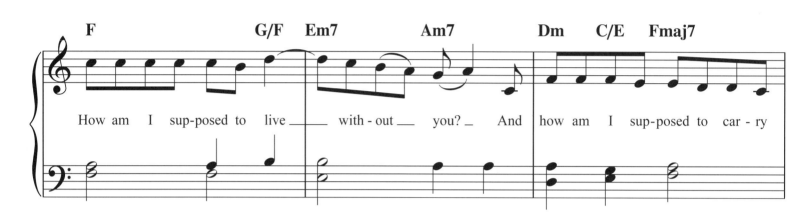

45

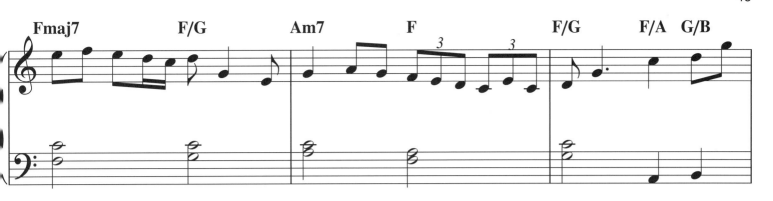

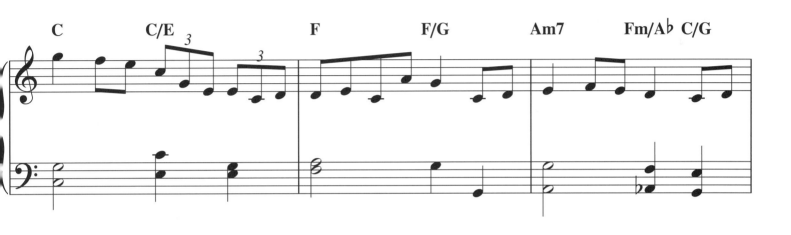

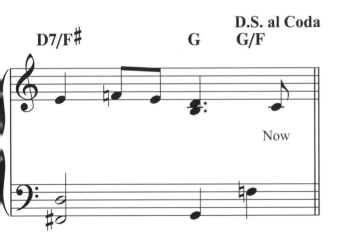

D.S. al Coda

Now

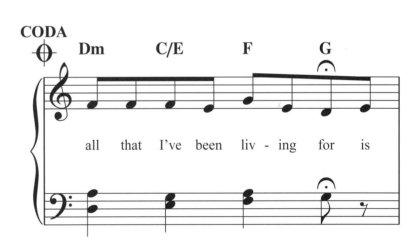

CODA

all that I've been liv-ing for is

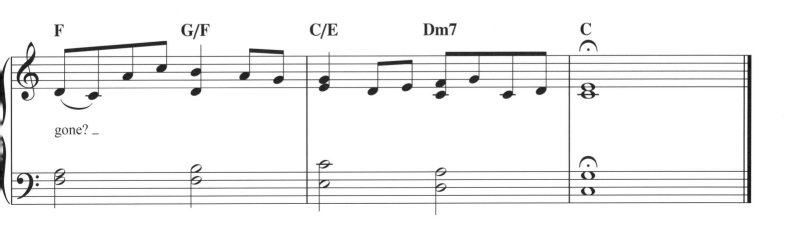

gone?

HOW WOULD YOU FEEL
(Paean)

Words and Music by
ED SHEERAN

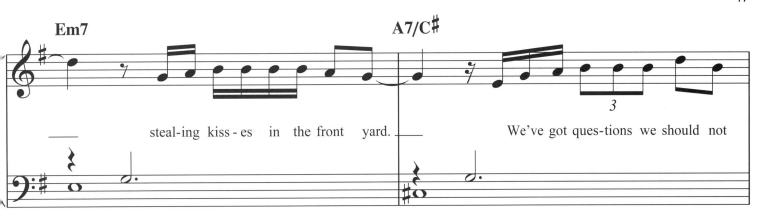

steal-ing kiss - es in the front yard. ___ We've got ques-tions we should not

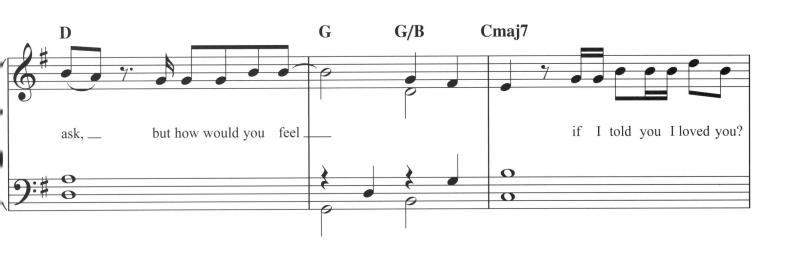

ask, __ but how would you feel ___ if I told you I loved you?

It's just some-thing that I want to do. ___

I'll be tak-ing my time, spend-ing my life ___ fall-ing deep-er in love with you. _

So tell me that you love me too.

So tell me that you love me too.

So tell me that you love me too.

rit.

Additional Lyrics

2. In the summer as the lilacs bloom
   Love flows deeper than a river
   Ev'ry moment I spend with you.
   We were sat upon our best friend's roof,
   I had both of my arms 'round you
   Watching the sunrise replace the moon.
   How would you feel
   If I told you I loved you?

IMAGINE

Words and Music by
JOHN LENNON

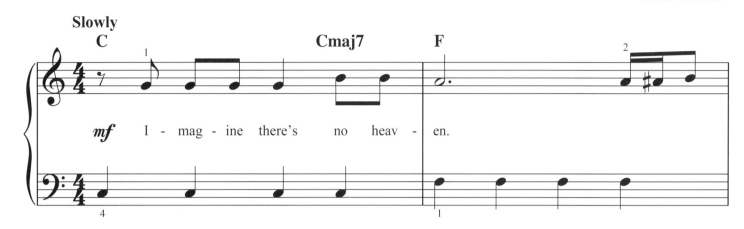

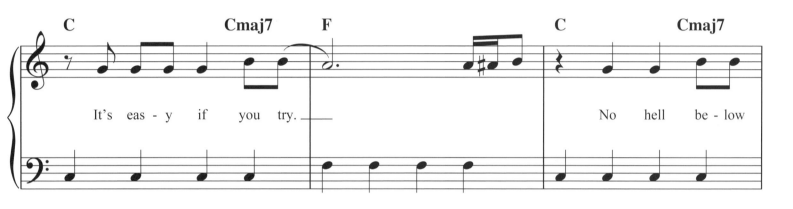

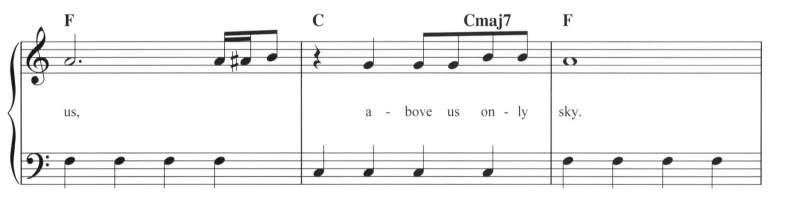

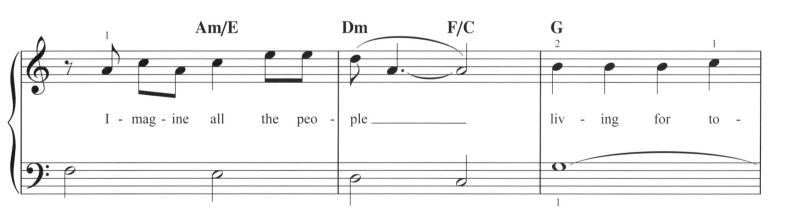

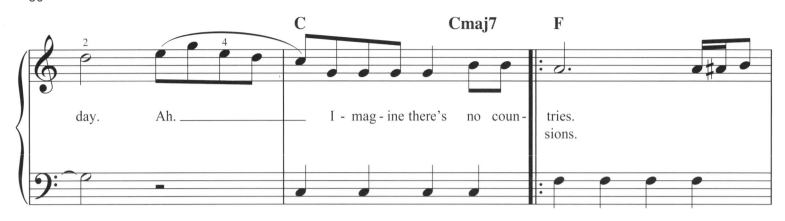

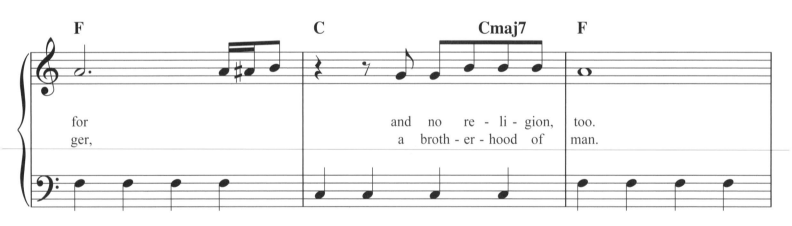

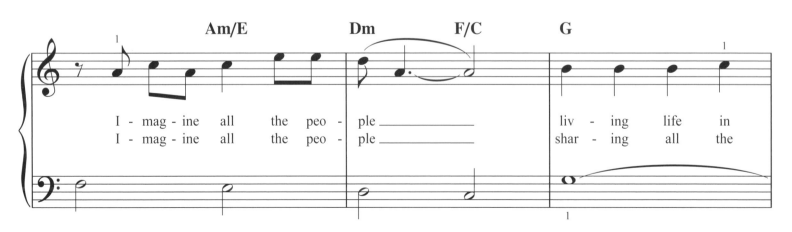

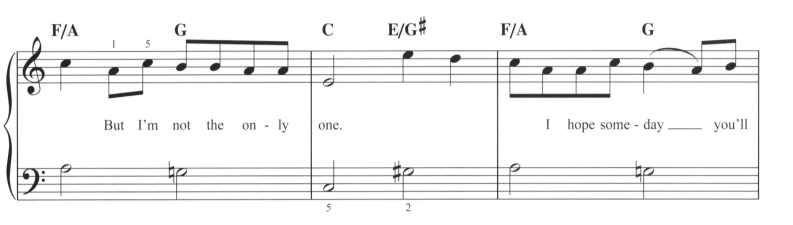

I WILL REMEMBER YOU

Theme from THE BROTHERS McMULLEN

Words and Music by SARAH McLACHLAN,
SEAMUS EGAN and DAVE MERENDA

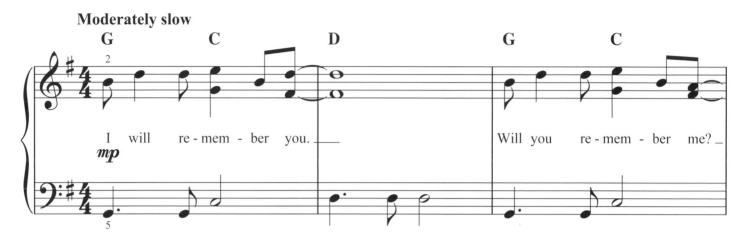

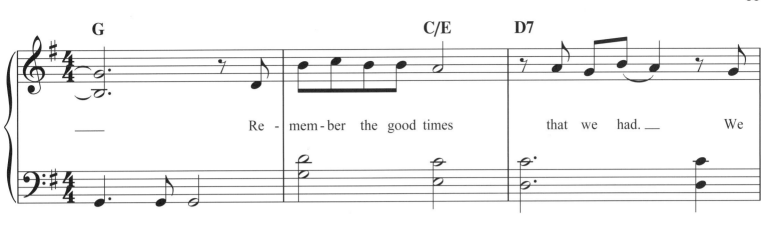

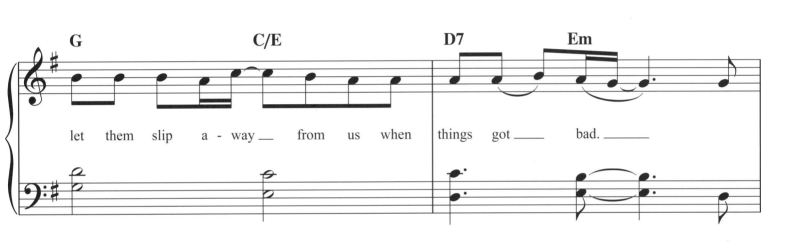

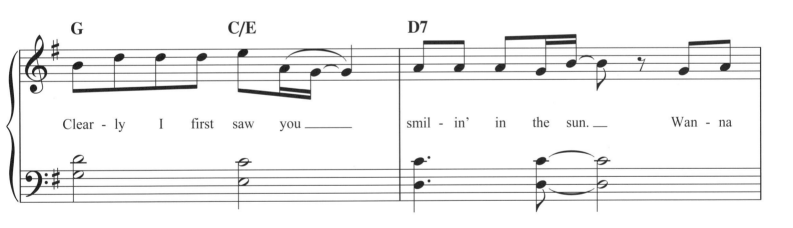

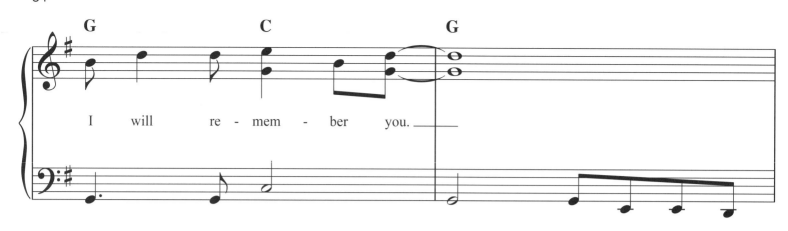

I will re - mem - ber you.

Will you re - mem - ber me? Don't let your life ___

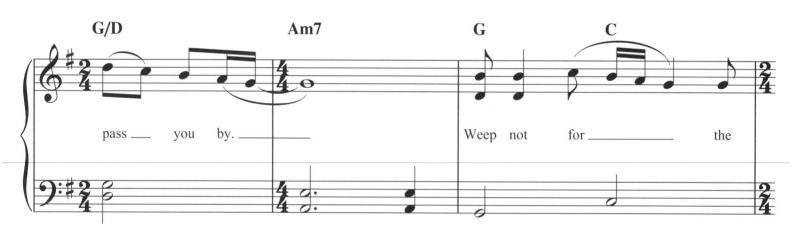

pass ___ you by. ___ Weep not for ___ the

mem - o - ries. ___ I will re - mem - ber you. _

55

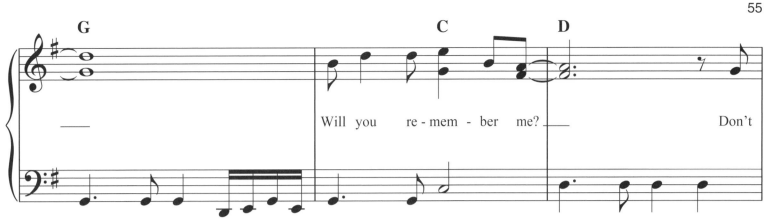

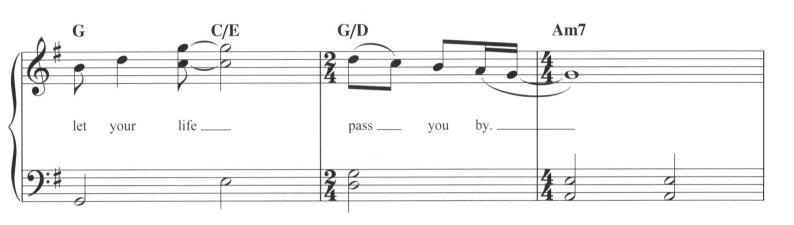

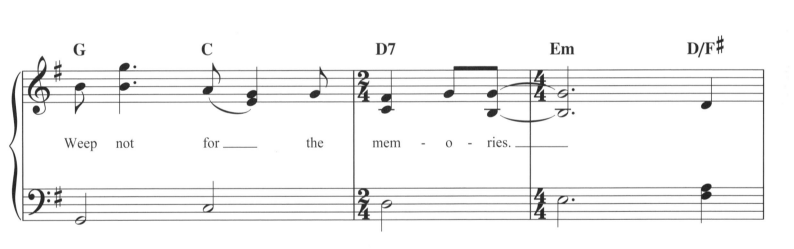

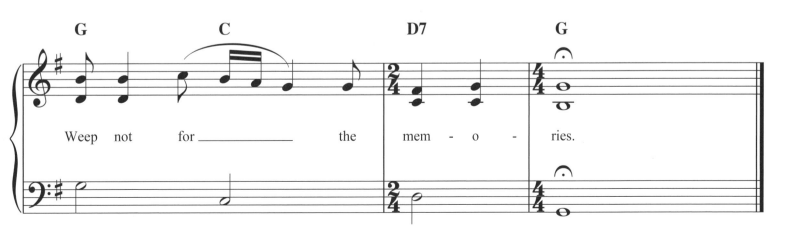

THE LUCKIEST

Words and Music by
BEN FOLDS

Freely with sentiment

1. I don't get man-y things right the first time. In
2.-3. *(See additional lyrics)*

fact, I am told that a lot. Now I know all ___ the wrong turns, ___ the

stum - bles ___ and falls brought ___ me here.

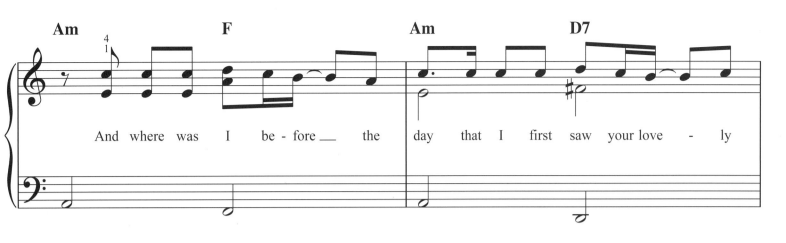

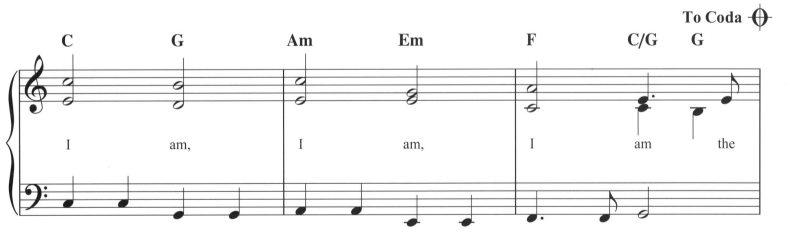

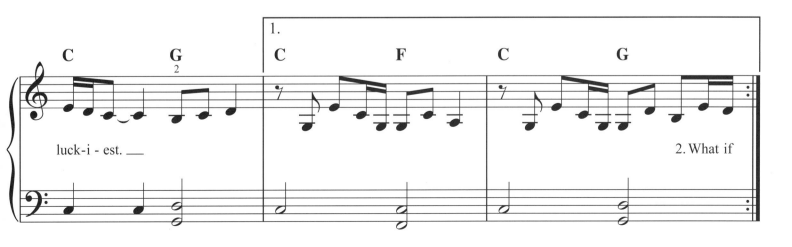

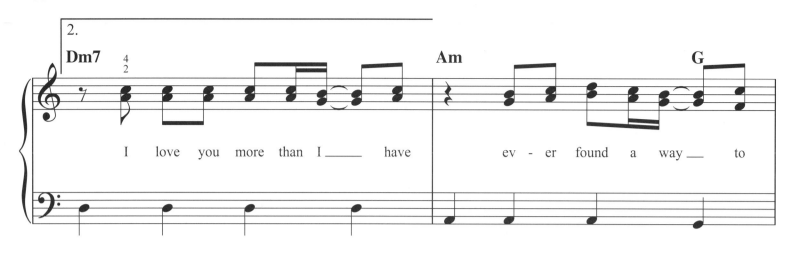

I love you more than I _____ have ev - er found a way ___ to

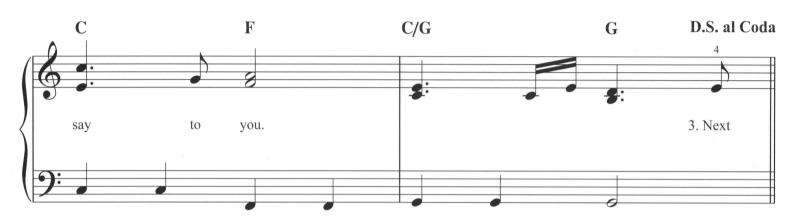

say to you. 3. Next

luck - i - est. ___ rit.

Additional Lyrics

2. What if I'd been born fifty years before you
   In a house on the street where you live?
   Maybe I'd be outside as you passed on your bike,
   Would I know?
   In a wide sea of eyes I see one pair that I recognize
   And I know that I am, I am, I am the luckiest.

3. Next door there's an old man who lived into his nineties
   And one day passed away in his sleep.
   And his wife, she stayed for a couple of days
   And passed away. I'm sorry I know
   That's a strange way to tell you that I know we belong,
   That I know that I am, I am, I am the luckiest.

PIANO MAN

Words and Music by
BILLY JOEL

C/G   F   G7sus   C

mak - in' love to his ton - ic and gin.

F/C   Cmaj7   G7   C

He says, "Son, can you

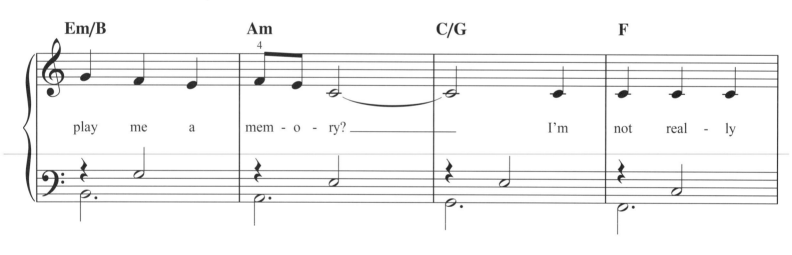

Em/B   Am   C/G   F

play me a mem - o - ry? I'm not real - ly

C/E   D   G7   C

sure how it goes, but it's sad and it's

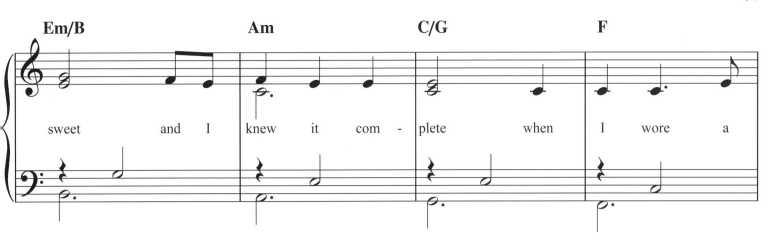

sweet and I knew it com - plete when I wore a

young - er man's clothes." Da da

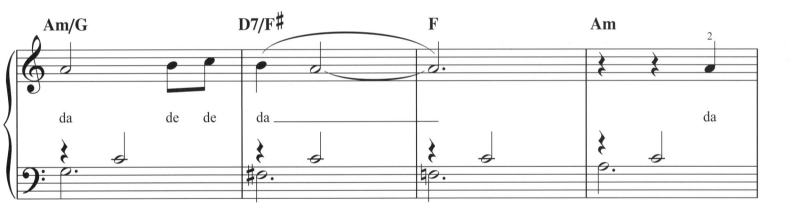

da de de da da

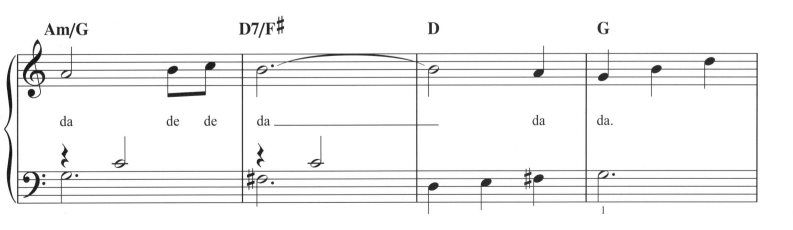

da de de da da da.

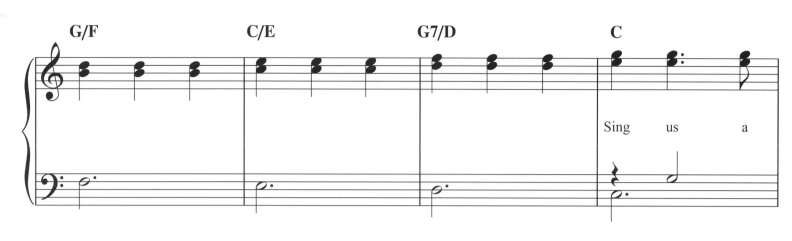

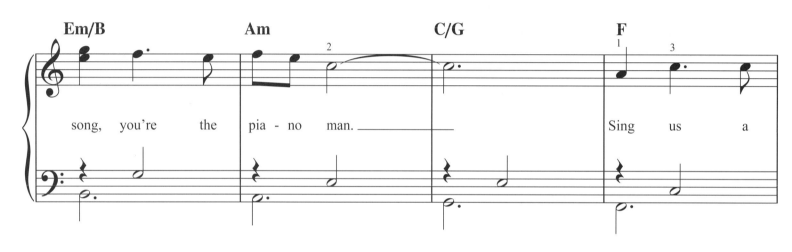

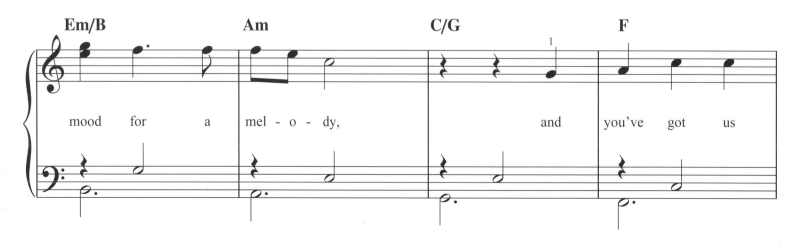

63

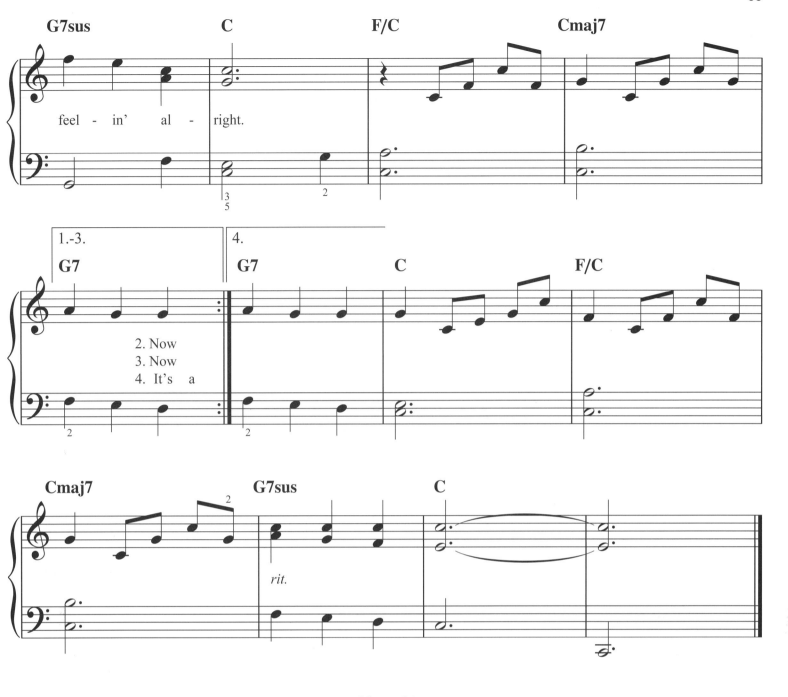

Additional Lyrics

2. Now John at the bar is a friend of mine,
   He gets me my drinks for free,
   And he's quick with a joke or to light up your smoke,
   But there's someplace that he'd rather be.
   He says, "Bill, I believe this is killing me,"
   As a smile ran away from his face.
   "Well, I'm sure that I could be a movie star
   If I could get out of this place."
   Chorus

3. Now Paul is a real estate novelist
   Who never had time for a wife,
   And he's talkin' with Davy who's still in the Navy
   And probably will be for life.
   And the waitress is practicing politics
   As the businessmen slowly get stoned.
   Yes, they're sharing a drink they call loneliness,
   But it's better than drinkin' alone.
   Chorus

4. It's a pretty good crowd for a Saturday,
   And the manager gives me a smile
   'Cause he knows that it's me they've been comin' to see
   To forget about life for a while.
   And the piano sounds like a carnival,
   And the microphone smells like a beer,
   And they sit at the bar and put bread in my jar
   And say, "Man, what are you doin' here?"
   Chorus

RIBBON IN THE SKY

Words and Music by
STEVIE WONDER

Slowly, with expression

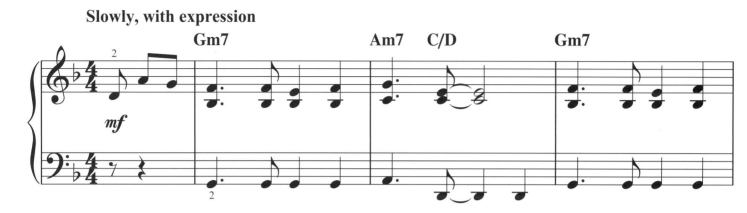

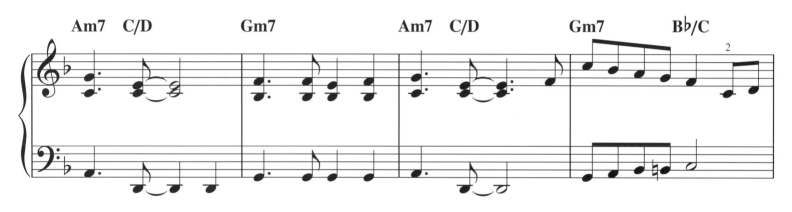

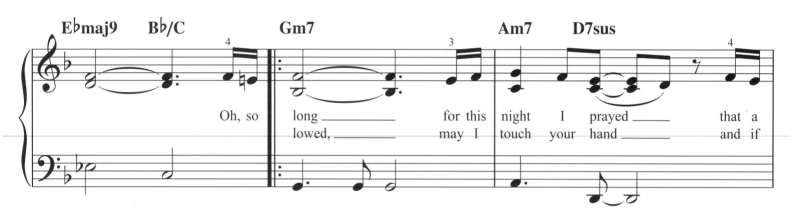

Oh, so long _____ for this night I prayed _____ that a
lowed, _____ may I touch your hand _____ and if

star _____ would guide you my way _____ to share with _____ me this
pleased _____ may I once a - gain _____ so that you _____ too will

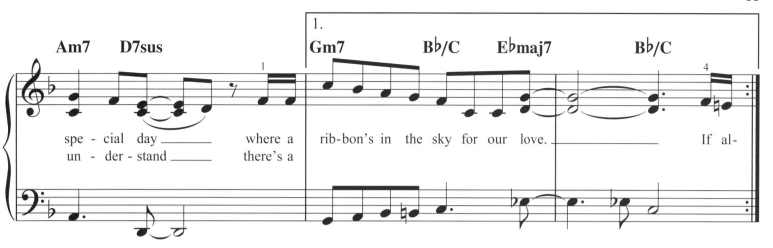

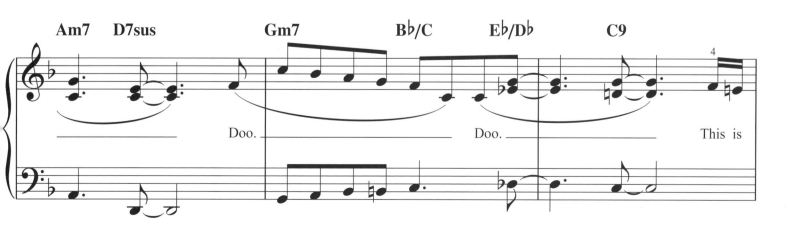

66

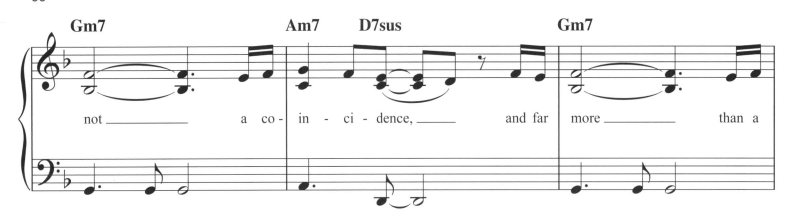

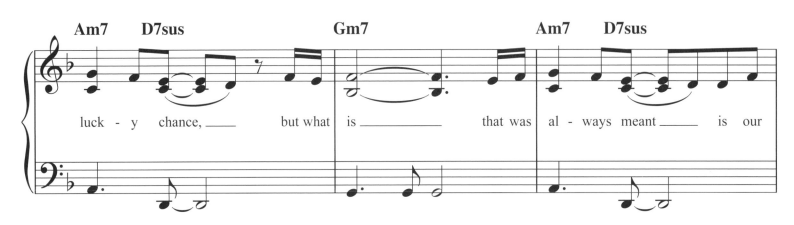

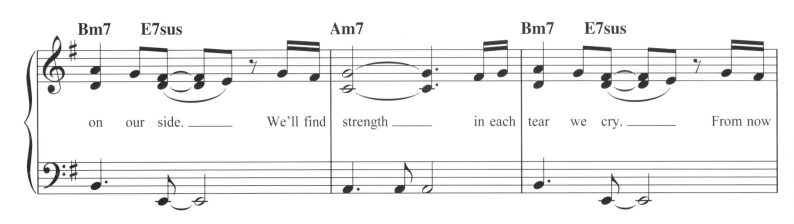

on _____ it will be you and I _____ and our rib - bon in the sky,

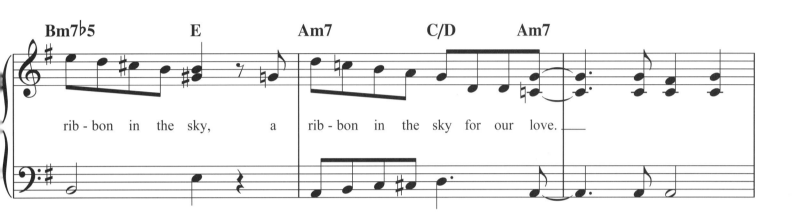

rib - bon in the sky, a rib - bon in the sky for our love. _____

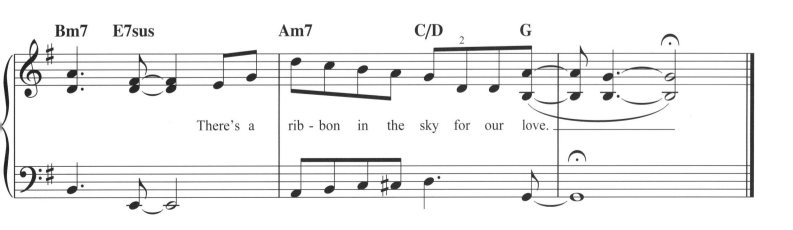

There's a rib - bon in the sky for our love. _____

SEE YOU AGAIN
from FURIOUS 7

Words and Music by CAMERON THOMAZ,
CHARLIE PUTH, JUSTIN FRANKS,
ANDREW CEDAR, DANN HUME,
JOSH HARDY and PHOEBE COCKBURN

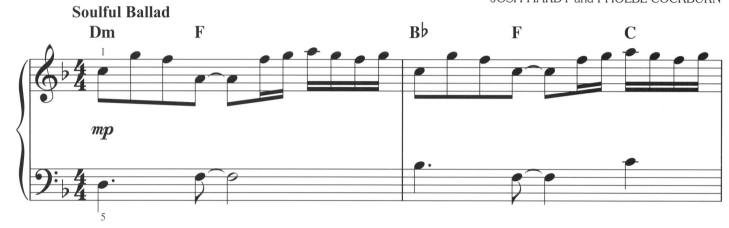

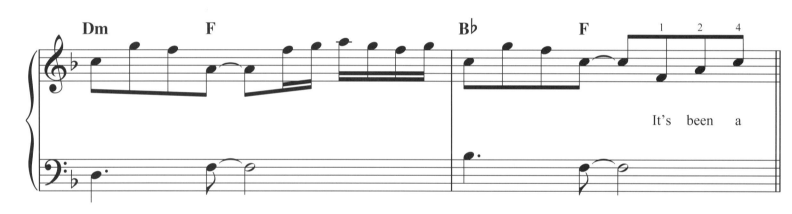

It's been a

long day ___ with- out you, my friend. ___ And I'll tell you all a- bout it when I

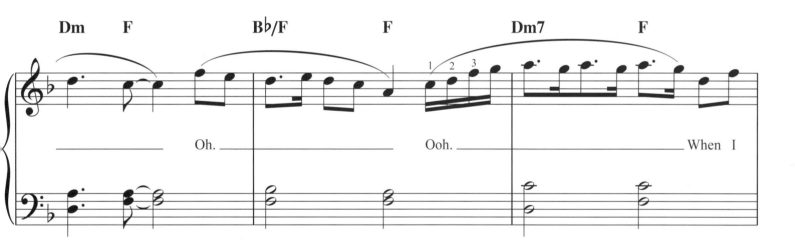

So let the

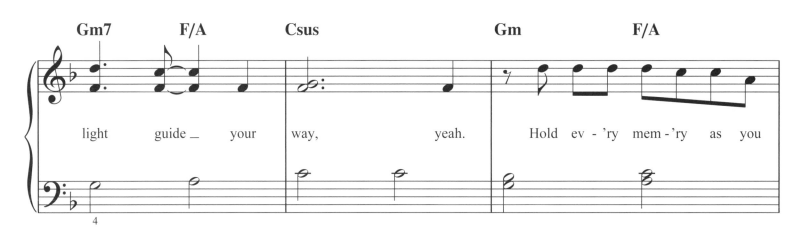

light guide __ your way, yeah. Hold ev-'ry mem-'ry as you

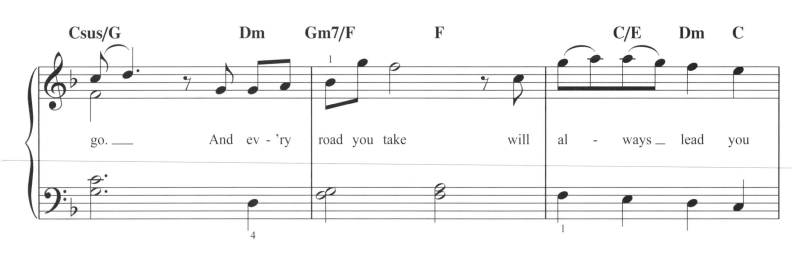

go. __ And ev-'ry road you take will al - ways __ lead you

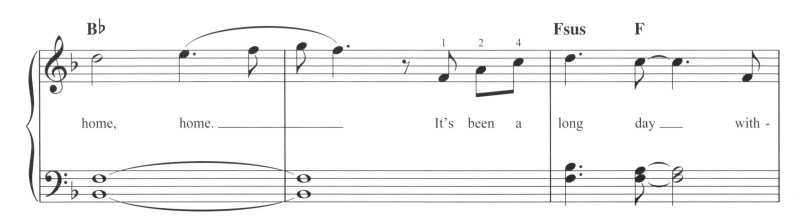

home, home. __ It's been a long day __ with -

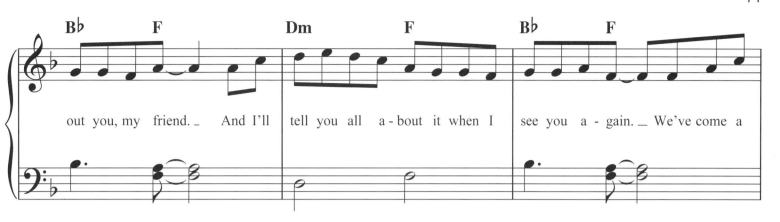

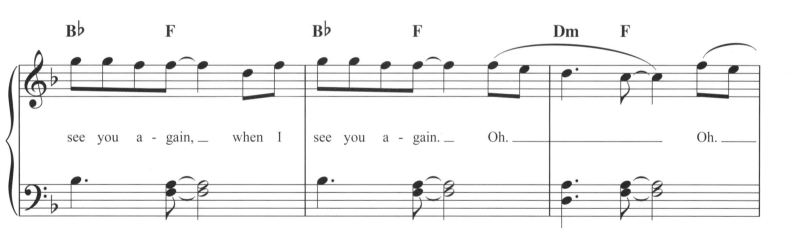

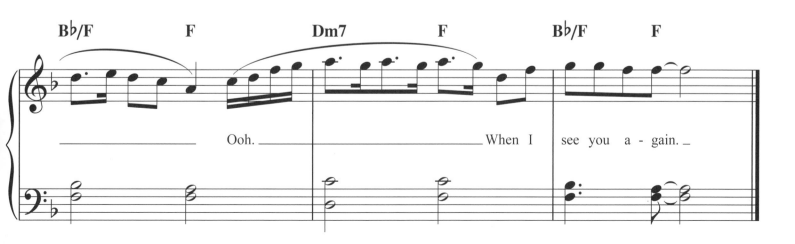

SO FAR AWAY

Words and Music by
CAROLE KING

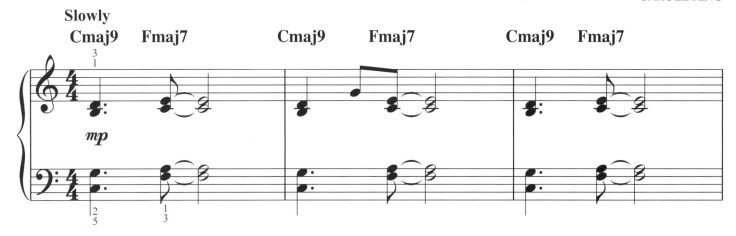

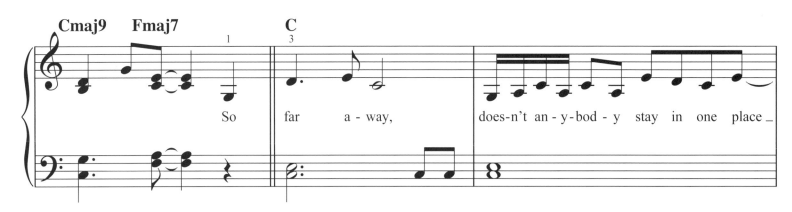

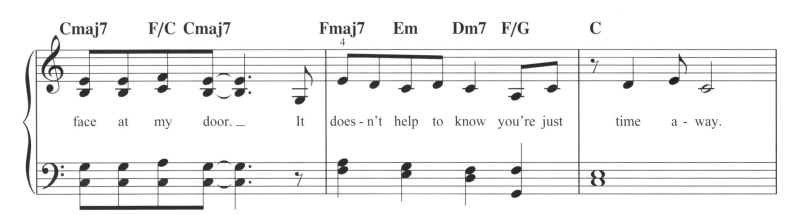

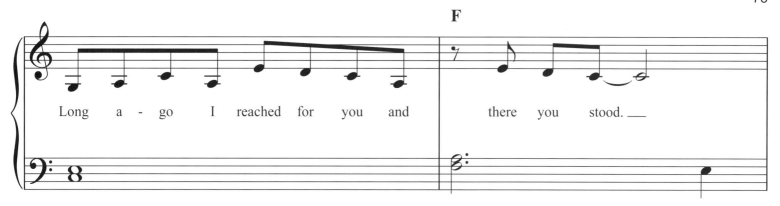

Long a - go I reached for you and there you stood. ___

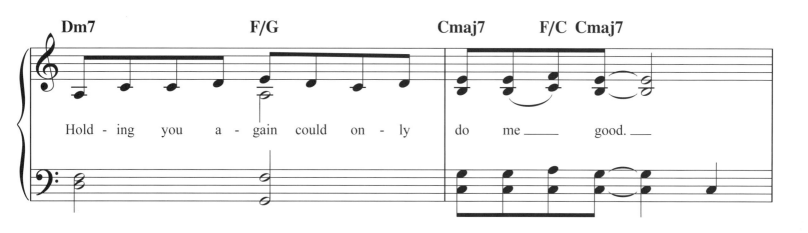

Hold - ing you a - gain could on - ly do me ___ good. ___

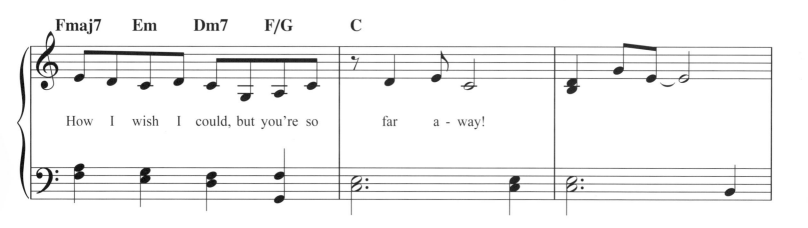

How I wish I could, but you're so far a - way!

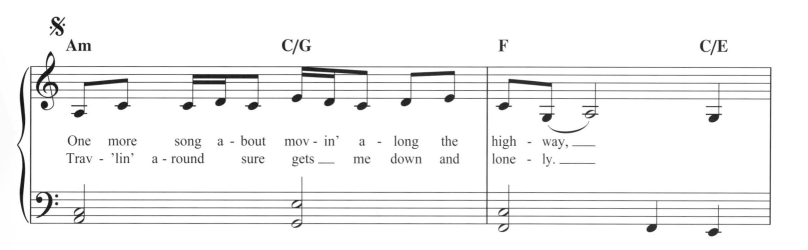

One more song a - bout mov - in' a - long the high - way, ___
Trav - 'lin' a - round sure gets ___ me down and lone - ly. ___

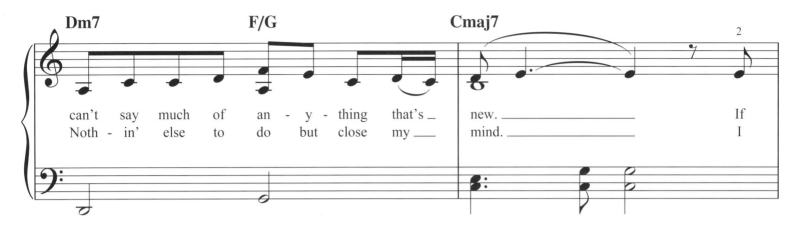

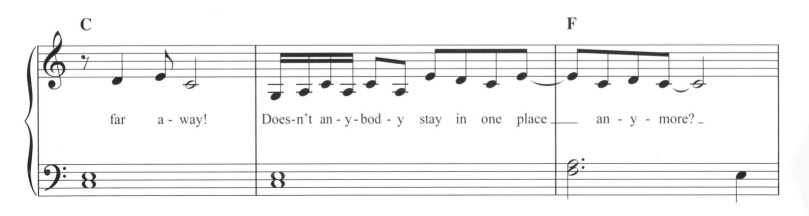

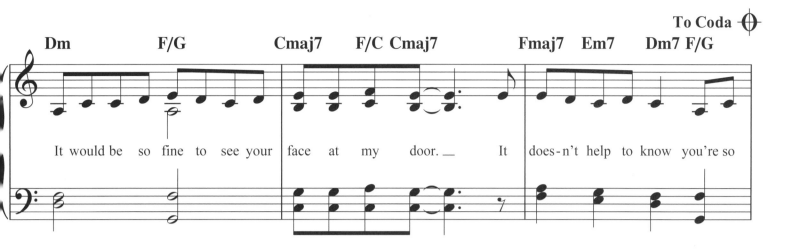

To Coda

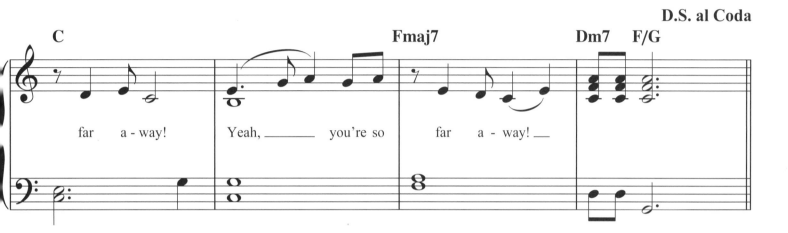

D.S. al Coda

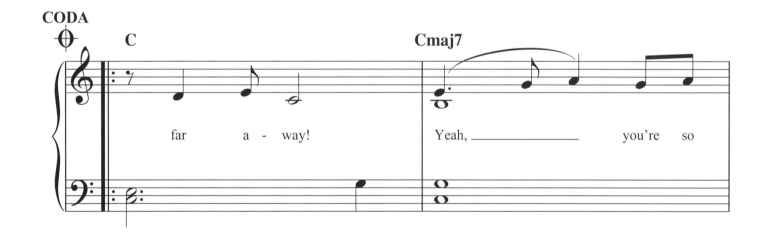

STAY WITH ME

Words and Music by SAM SMITH,
JAMES NAPIER, WILLIAM EDWARD PHILLIPS,
TOM PETTY and JEFF LYNNE

78

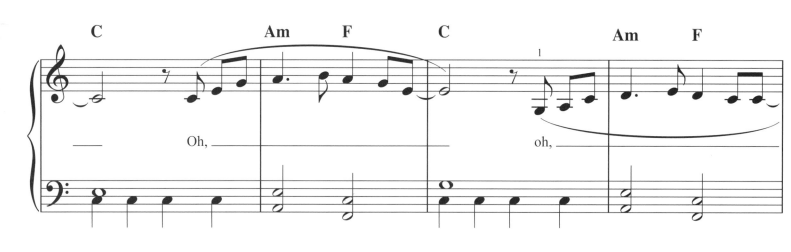

WONDERFUL TONIGHT

Words and Music by
ERIC CLAPTON

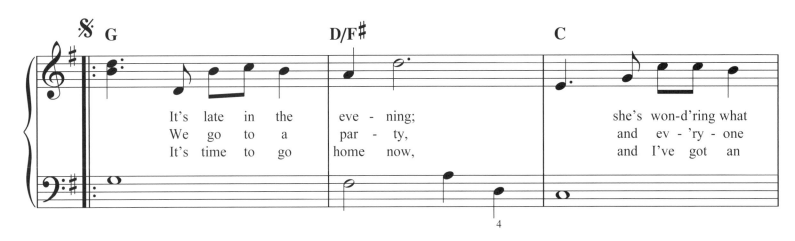

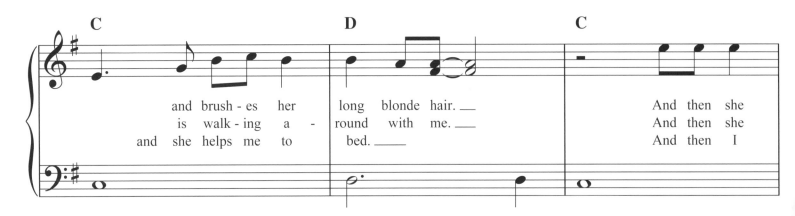

D   G   D/F♯   Em   C

asks me,   "Do I look all   right?"   And I say, "Yes,   you look
asks me,   "Do you feel all   right?"   And I say, "Yes,   I feel
tell her,   as I turn out the   light,   I say, "My   dar- ling, you are

D   To Coda ⊕ | 1. G   D/F♯   C

won-der - ful to -   night."
won-der - ful to -
won-der - ful to -

D   2. G   C

night."   I feel   won - der - ful ___ be -

D   G   D/F♯   Em   C

cause I see ___ the   love light in ___ your   eyes.   Then the   won - der of it

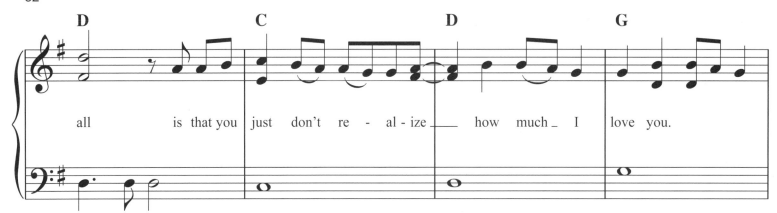

all   is that you just don't re - al - ize ___ how much _ I   love you.

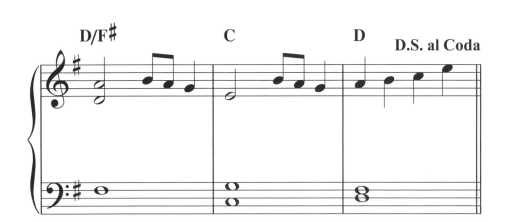

D.S. al Coda

CODA

night."

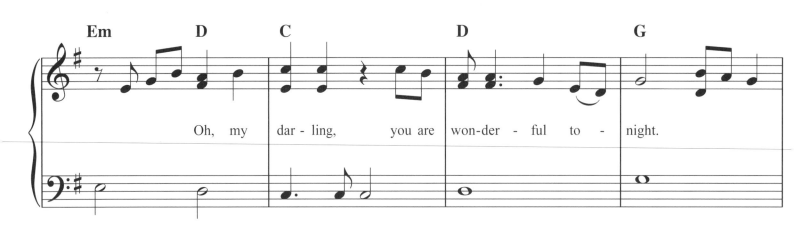

Oh, my   dar - ling,   you are won-der - ful to - night.

rit.

THE WAY WE WERE

from the Motion Picture THE WAY WE WERE

Words by ALAN and MARILYN BERGMAN
Music by MARVIN HAMLISCH

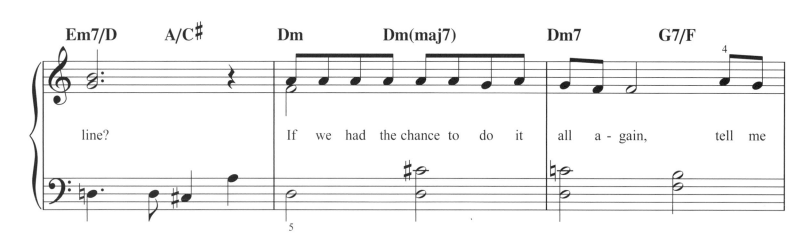

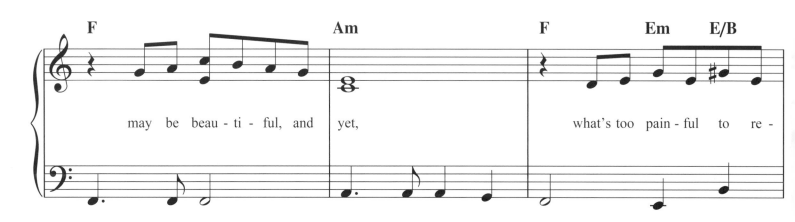

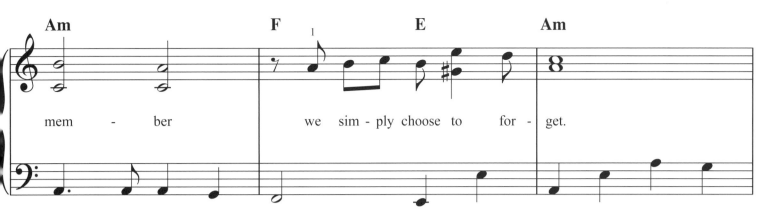

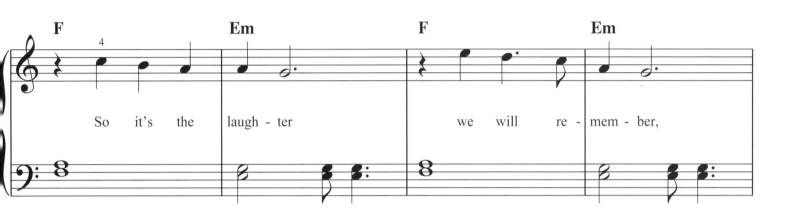

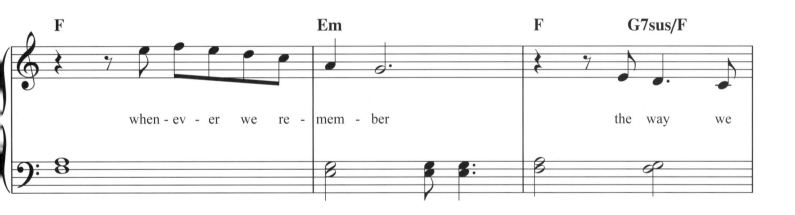

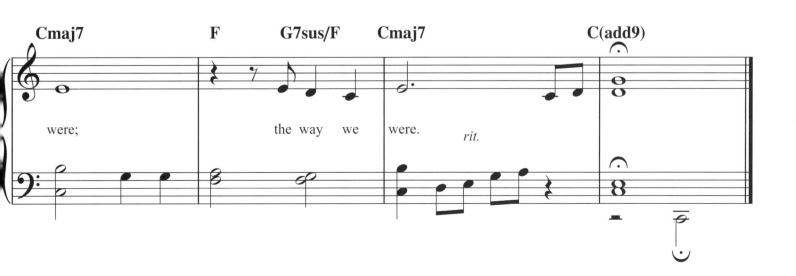

WHEN I WAS YOUR MAN

Words and Music by BRUNO MARS,
ARI LEVINE, PHILIP LAWRENCE
and ANDREW WYATT

Same bed, but it feels just a lit - tle bit big - ger now. _____

My pride, my ___ e - go, my needs and my self - ish ways _____

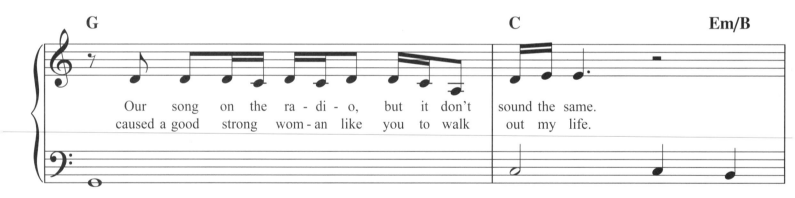

Our song on the ra - di - o, but it don't sound the same.

caused a good strong wom - an like you to walk out my life.

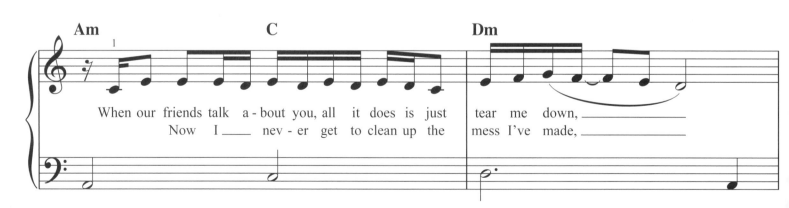

When our friends talk a - bout you, all it does is just tear me down, _____

Now I ___ nev - er get to clean up the mess I've made, _____

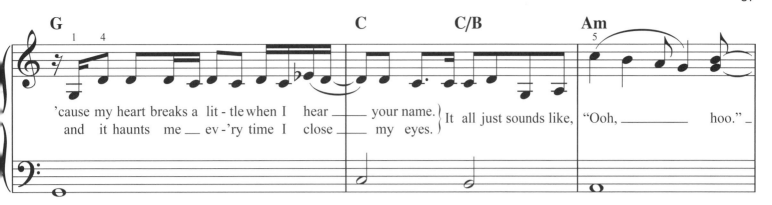

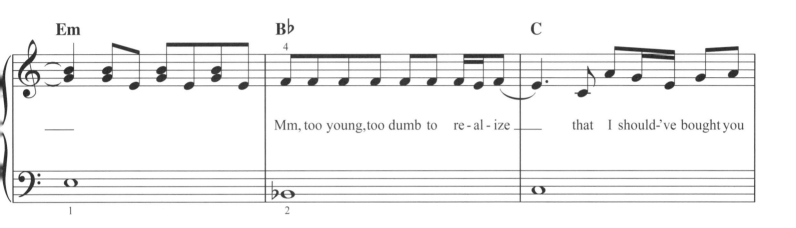

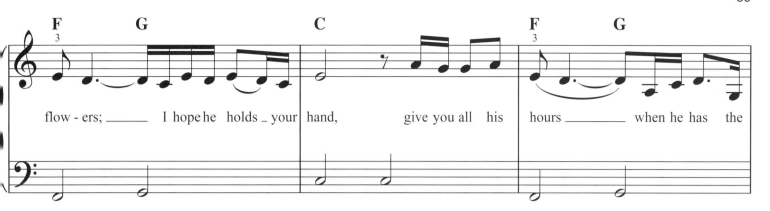

flow - ers; _____ I hope he holds _ your hand, give you all his hours _____ when he has the

chance; take you to ev - 'ry par - ty, ___ 'cause I re-mem-ber how much _ you love

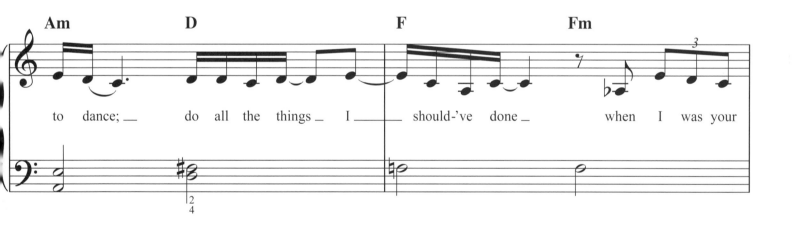

to dance; _ do all the things _ I ____ should-'ve done _ when I was your

man. Do all the things I ____ should-'ve done when I was your man.

rit.

YOU'VE GOT A FRIEND

Words and Music by
CAROLE KING

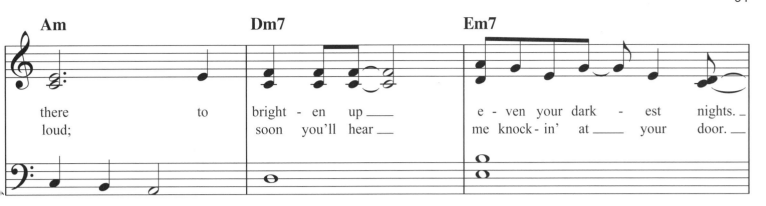

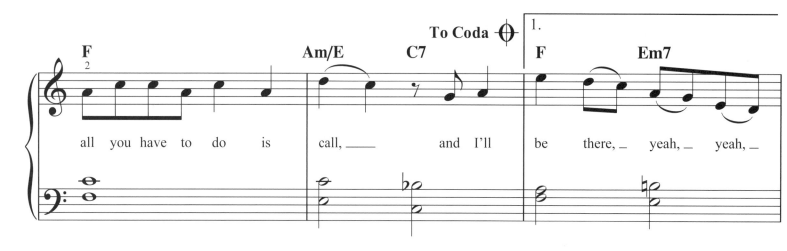

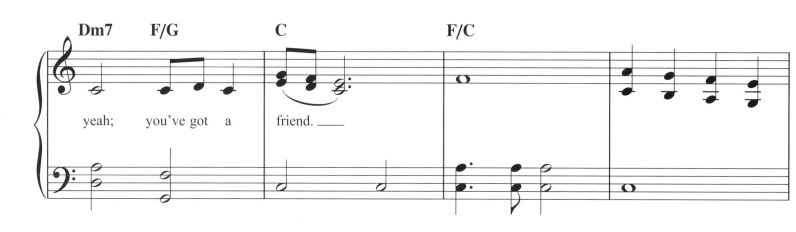

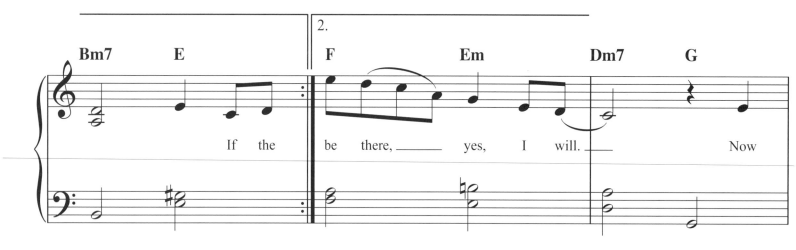

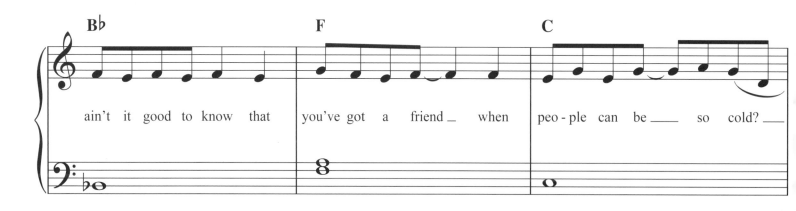

93

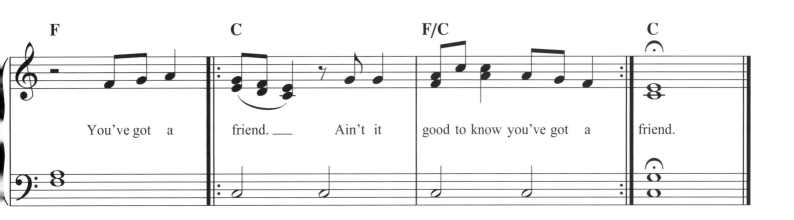

YOUR SONG

Words and Music by ELTON JOHN
and BERNIE TAUPIN

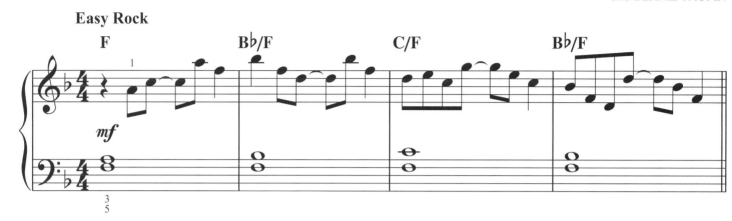

It's a lit-tle bit
If I were a
fun-ny,
sculp-tor,
this feel-ing in-
but then a-gain,
side; ___
no, ___

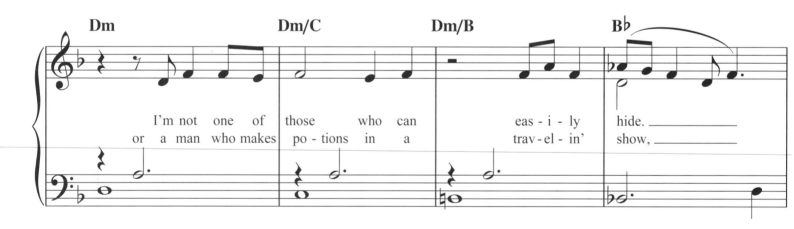

I'm not one of
or a man who makes
those who can
po-tions in a
eas-i-ly
trav-el-in'
hide. ___
show, ___

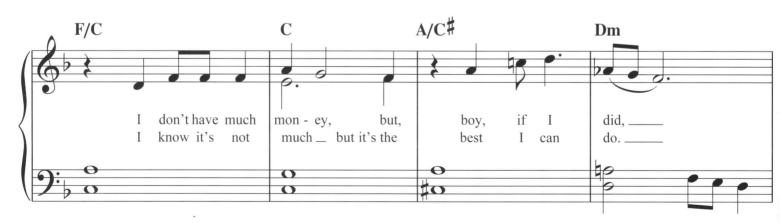

I don't have much
I know it's not
mon-ey, but,
much __ but it's the
boy, if I
best I can
did, ___
do. ___

I hope you don't mind, I hope you don't mind that I put down in ____

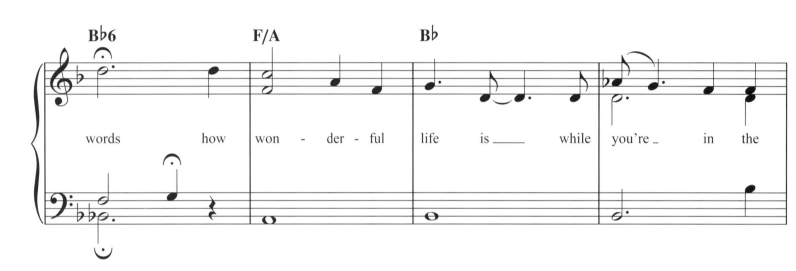

words how won - der - ful life is ____ while you're _ in the

world.

rit.